THE EUCHARIST
FOR BEGINNERS

SACRAMENT, SACRIFICE, AND COMMUNION

THE EUCHARIST FOR BEGINNERS

SACRAMENT, SACRIFICE, AND COMMUNION

Kenneth J. Howell

CATHOLIC ANSWERS
San Diego
2006

Unless otherwise noted, Scripture quotations are taken from the
Revised Standard Version: Catholic Edition (RSV:CE) of the Bible,
copyright © 1996 by the Division of Christian Education of the National
Council of Churches of Christ in the United States of America.

Published by Catholic Answers, Inc.
P.O. Box 199000
San Diego, California 92159-9000
(888) 291-8000 (U.S. orders)
(619) 387-7200 (international orders)
(619) 387-0042 (fax)
www.catholic.com (web)

Nihil Obstat: I have concluded that the materials
presented in this work are free of doctrinal and moral errors.
Imprimatur: Permission to publish this work is granted.
Most Reverend Daniel R. Jenky, C.S.C., Bishop of Peoria, October 26, 2006

Cover by Devin Schadt
Interior design by Claudine Mansour Design
Printed in the United States of America
ISBN: 1-933919-01-9

Dedicated to Sharon,
My Beloved Companion

CONTENTS

Part One

THE EUCHARIST AS SACRAMENT

1

THE EUCHARIST: A SUPPER FOR LOVERS

Love is man's origin,
Love is his constant calling,
Love is his fulfillment in heaven.

THESE THREE SHORT LINES from the Mass for a wedding express the essence of the Catholic faith. There's no greater calling than to learn to love God and our fellow human beings. It is a lifelong journey, but to fill every moment of our day with love requires more than we can deliver. Even so, this prayer reminds us that it is our true nature to love, because love is the origin from which we came.

I chose that quote to begin this book because this is a love story. It's about the love Jesus has for us—for you—in the Eucharist. Christ wants to win our hearts so that we might return the love he has shown us. All his life and ministry had this one purpose: that we might believe and trust him as our Redeemer and Lord, that we might love him, the source of all love.

What does he want for you, his beloved brother or sister? To return to the one source that can fulfill our human nature: God's love. Learning how to love is our constant calling; it is the goal of our lives. And it is why Jesus left us the greatest banquet table ever set. The Eucharist is his gift of love to you.

UNDERSTANDING JESUS' DESIRE

We know about the institution of the Eucharist—the Last Supper, which was the first "Mass"—because three evangelists and the great missionary apostle Paul wrote about it (Matt. 26:26–30; (Mark 14:22–25; Luke 22:15–20; 1 Cor. 11:23–26). There also are other verses that allude to it (1 Cor. 5:7; 10:16–17). Among all these writers, it is Luke who stresses how much Jesus wanted to celebrate that meal with his apostles:

> And they [the disciples] went, and found it [the upper room] as he had told them; and they prepared the passover. And when the hour came, he sat at table, and the apostles with him. And he said to them, "I have earnestly desired to eat this passover with you before I suffer; for I tell you I shall not eat it until it is fulfilled in the kingdom of God (Luke 22:13–16).

Luke's description is unique because he tells us explicitly of Jesus' longing. It is expressed with the unusual words "I have earnestly

---

To Show Our Gratitude

Eucharist: The term comes from the Greek word *eucharistia*, meaning "thanksgiving" or "gratitude." While *eucharistia* is used in the Bible and in early Christian writings with this broad meaning, it quickly became a technical term for the celebration that Paul calls "the Lord's supper" (1 Cor. 11:20).

Outside the New Testament, one of the earliest accounts of this celebration is in a document called the *Didache* (meaning "teaching") or *Teaching of the Twelve Apostles*, which was written in the late first century. Its author says, "Now concerning the Eucharist, give thanks [*eucharistesate*] like this," and proceeds with a Eucharistic prayer. It is clear the writer is aware of the connection between the technical term   and the root meaning of the verb for "to give thanks." Why "thanksgiving"? Because the most important response to Jesus' gift of love is gratitude. We want to love him because he first loved us (1 John 4:19).

---

desired to eat this passover." In the original Greek, "I have earnestly desired" is *epithumia epethumesa*. Literally, that is more of a Hebrew or Aramaic manner of speaking—"with desire I desire"—not a typical Greek way of speaking. This Semitic phrasing sounds odd. The conjecture that this usage is due to Luke, however, is not certain. Luke may have used it because Jesus' words were reported to him in a Semitic phrasing, and he may simply reflect that.

Why does this matter? Luke, a physician, was an educated person who wrote beautiful Greek prose, but sometimes he adopted Semitic ways of speech to bring life and color to his descriptions. In this verse, he wants to put us right there with Jesus by using a Semitic mode of speech. A looser, a more vivid translation of that phrase might be "I have longed with everything within me to eat this Passover with you." The evangelist, inspired by the Holy Spirit, wanted us to know how Jesus felt about his last Passover.

Why was this meal so important for our Lord? Luke 22:15 tells us that Jesus knew he was going to leave his disciples. He had spent three years with them, sharing common meals, sleeping in the open, ministering to the crowds, and, most of all, teaching and healing. No doubt part of his feelings that night was an intense sorrow, because he knew he would not be with them in the same way much longer. Another reason for Jesus' desire was his love for his disciples. He wanted to comfort them, because they probably still did not understand that his mission as Messiah meant his suffering. Perhaps they hoped that he would avert the dangers facing him and be able to establish the kingdom of God without his own demise. If they did not comprehend his suffering, that would have only intensified the pain in his heart. But neither of these reasons gets to the core of Jesus' overwhelming desire to share this last meal with his closest friends.

We need to keep in mind that this was not just *any* meal. This was the most important dinner of the year for the Jews. It was Passover. All three synoptic Gospels identify it as the annual Passover meal the Jews were obliged to celebrate (Matt. 26:17; Mark 14:12; Luke 22:1). It is hard for Western non-Jews to fully appreciate how meaningful this night would have been for Christ and his disciples.

To better understand Jesus' desire on that evening requires a look at the meaning of Passover.

THE PASSOVER: A SPECIAL MEAL FOR GOD'S PEOPLE

Exodus 12 gives an account of the first Passover on the night of the flight from Egypt. Deuteronomy 16:1–8 offers instructions for the repetition of the feast in Israel's later history. A combined reading of these texts indicates several important features.

Passover as memorial. First and foremost, the Passover was to be a perpetual memorial. Exodus 12:14 calls it a "memorial day" for all of Israel's generations. Deuteronomy 16 also emphasizes the perpetual character of this celebration by enshrining the practice as an annual feast. There were several reasons for making it a yearly requirement. One of the most important had to do with teaching children:

> You shall observe this rite as an ordinance for you and for your sons for ever. And when you come to the land which the Lord will give you, as he has promised, you shall keep this service. And when your children say to you, 'What do you mean by this service?' you shall say, 'It is the sacrifice of the Lord's passover, for he passed over the houses of the people of Israel in Egypt, when he slew the Egyptians but spared our houses.'" And the people bowed their heads and worshiped (Ex. 12:24–27).

By an annual celebration, the children of Israel of succeeding generations would learn of, and participate in, the original Passover. By the regular repetition of this ordinance, the Israelites would learn its intrinsic significance. The question and answer between children and adults described in these verses indicates that the sacrifice had to be continued so that God's people would never forget the Lord's goodness to them. As Israel's historic experience later proved, God's redeemed children can easily forget the wonders that he does. They need something tangible and concrete in their lives to remain faithful to God. It was the sacrifice of the Passover that helped keep God's love repeatedly before them.

Passover and the blood of the lamb. A second theme in the Passover story has to do with the blood of the lamb. What did that sacrifice remind them of? It never allowed them to forget the great lengths to which God went to save them from slavery and judgment. The blood of the sacrificial lamb protected them from the avenging angel:

> It is the Lord's Passover. For I will pass through the land of Egypt that night, and I will smite all the first-born in the land of Egypt, both man and beast; and on all the gods of Egypt I will execute judgments: I am the Lord. The blood shall be a sign for you, upon the houses where you are; and when I see the blood, I will pass over you, and no plague shall fall upon you to destroy you, when I smite the land of Egypt (Ex. 12:11–13).

How could the blood on the doorposts shield the people inside the house? At an explicit level, the text says that it acted as an *indicator* as to who was in the house, so the angel would not strike the blood-stained homes. But behind this simple sign there is more. The blood came from the lamb that was slain by the members of the household inside and therefore represented a bond between the blood outside and the people inside.

Throughout the ancient world, including Israel, people identified with the god to whom they sacrificed. For example, Paul says that there can be no association or agreement between false gods and a Christian (2 Cor. 6:14–18). He argues that sacrifice in a pagan temple identifies the worshiper with that false god. Similarly, the blood on the doors of the Israelites associated them with the protective sacrifice from which the blood came. This distinguished the people of Israel from the Egyptians. The yearly sacrifice of Passover reminded the Israelites of how God had set them apart from the world. The blood showed that these people were identified with the true God.

Passover as purity. A third theme in the Passover story is purity. The lamb sacrificed had to be a one-year-old male without blemish (Ex. 12:5). The sacrifice had to be pure, or it wouldn't be acceptable to God—*and* the people themselves had to be pure as well. No doubt, that is the meaning behind having only unleavened bread in the house (Ex. 12:15, 17, 19–20). Carefully removing all leavened bread on the first day for the feast indicates that the purification of the house was to be a deliberate choice and effort (Ex. 12:15). This aspect was so important that the Passover also came to be called the Feast of Unleavened Bread (Ex. 12:17; Deut. 16:16).

Another way in which purity is woven into the account is the requirements for who can eat the Passover sacrifice. There are two sides to this law. One stresses that only one who is circumcised may take part, because circumcision functioned as an outward sign of accepting God's covenant (Gen. 17:1–14; Ex. 12:43–49). It meant belonging to the people of God. If an alien, traditionally called a sojourner, circumcised his family, he and they would be regarded as ritually pure and belonging to Israel. The other side of the requirement that only God's people eat of the Passover lamb is that it gave them a sense of identity. It was "the whole assembly of the congregation of Israel," which was to sacrifice the lamb on the fourteenth day of the month (Ex. 12:6). By identifying with the paschal lamb, each participant would learn of being within God's people as a child of God. This identity came from the gracious love of God.

So Passover gave protection, salvation, and identity to the Jews and to those who joined them through the rite of circumcision. The sacrifice of the lamb was the central act around which everything else revolved. And the subsequent history of the Passover in post-biblical Judaism demonstrates that it continued as the central celebration of the year that instilled in the people of Israel:

• a sense of gratitude to God for redemption,
• a sense of solidarity with their ancestors, and
• a sense of identity with all other Jews.

JESUS' INSTITUTION OF THE EUCHARIST

With a better understanding of the feast's background, you can see why every Passover meal was one rich in symbolism, history, tradition, and belief. The Last Supper was no exception. It seems safe to assume that all the rich meaning surrounding that gathering in the Upper Room must have been on Jesus' mind as he transformed the significance of that meal into something far greater than the Jews had ever known, something far greater than the world had ever known. What changed it? It was at this meal that a Passover celebrant declared, "This is my body. . . . This is the cup of my blood." Jesus' action transformed the annual marking of Passover from a pure symbol into a true sacramental participation in the divine life of God himself.

"This is my body. . . . This is the cup of my blood." What did Jesus mean by those key words? Since that night, millions of words have been written in an attempt to explain what our Lord said. Countless questions have been asked about what he did. Two key questions that arise are:

1. What is the significance of the occasion on which Jesus said these words?
2. What was his intention, especially with regard to the new community of faith he was establishing—that is, the Church?

The occasion, being the Passover, made it a special meal celebrating redemption. Jesus and his apostles would have been well aware of all its elements: sacrifice, memorial, annual renewal, purity of the lamb, protection of the blood, and identity with God's people. That has lead others—from New Testament authors to modern scholars—to believe that Jesus meant to infuse that meal with a much greater meaning.

Take, for example, the lamb of sacrifice. The New Testament picks up on this theme in several ways. Peter stresses the purity of Christ as the lamb:

> You know that you were ransomed from the futile ways inherited from your fathers, not with perishable things such as silver or gold, but with the precious blood of Christ, like that of a lamb without blemish or spot (1 Pet. 1:18–19).

Clearly, Peter is thinking of the purity of the Passover lamb as a foreshadowing of the truly Pure One, who is Christ. His contrast between precious metals (gold and silver) and Christ's blood is striking. We normally think of gold and silver as enduring, but Peter calls them "perishable" in comparison with the Lamb's blood because only this blood can last throughout eternity.

In a similar way, the author of the book of Hebrews refers to Christ's blood as obtaining "eternal redemption" (Heb. 9:12). The writer is not referring specifically to the Passover lamb, but he does stress the purity of Christ's self-sacrifice. That, much like the Passover, had to be pure:

> How much more shall the blood of Christ, who through the eternal Spirit offered himself without blemish to God, purify your conscience from dead works to serve the living God (Heb. 9:14).

And as is echoed at every Mass, John the Baptist speaks of Jesus as "the Lamb of God, who takes away the sin of the world" (John 1:29).

All these references to the lamb and to his blood suggest that the New Testament sees Christ as the fulfillment of the Passover lamb.

Our Treasure

"By giving the Eucharist the prominence it deserves, and by being careful not to diminish any of its dimensions or demands, we show that we are truly conscious of the greatness of this gift. We are urged to do so by an uninterrupted tradition, which from the first centuries on has found the Christian community ever vigilant in guarding this 'treasure.'"[1]

As Jesus celebrated his last Passover with his disciples, he knew that he was the lamb of God and that his death would atone for the world's sins. He wanted to connect that meal with his sacrifice on Calvary.

Beyond the significance of the occasion, what was Christ's intention in its celebration, especially with regard to this fledgling community of faith? That raises two questions:

1. When Jesus said, "This is my body," did he have any special desires for the Church that he established?
2. What is the connection between that Passover celebration and that Church?

The New Testament shows clearly that Jesus intended to establish a new people of God (Matt. 16:13–20; Eph. 2:20). All Christian history agrees that Jesus intended to have the Last Supper repeated after his return to heaven. In other words, this meal was the foundation of the Church's Eucharist. If this meal was to be the central feast of the Church, then it makes more sense that Jesus was establishing a new foundation by his words rather than just describing the bread or comparing it with his body. He meant his words to lay the foundation of the Church.

That connection—among the Passover, the Last Supper, and the Church—is confirmed when Paul says:

Cleanse out the old leaven that you may be a new lump, as you really are unleavened. For Christ, our paschal lamb, has been sacrificed. Let us, therefore, celebrate the festival, not with the old leaven, the leaven of malice and evil, but the unleavened bread of sincerity and truth (1 Cor. 5:7, 8).

In the context of 1 Corinthians 5, Paul uses this verse to exhort the Church, the new community of Christ, to discipline one of its members who is scandalizing the Church. He urges purity on the grounds that it is the new Israel celebrating the Passover with unleavened bread. Leaven, a symbol for sin, meant that the community had to be pure of heart in order to partake in the sacrifice of the Lamb of God, the lamb sacrificed for this feast being Christ himself.

The only celebration the Church could hold that is anything close to the Passover meal is the supper that Jesus established. Thus Paul is appealing to the eucharistic worship of the Church to urge the body of Christ toward purity. That eucharistic feast gives the Church its identity in the same way that the annual Passover gave an identity to the people of Israel. The New Testament sees Christ as the fulfillment of the Passover lamb and the supper he founded as the continuation of that ancient feast. The Eucharist is the "Passover" for the New Covenant people of God, the Church.

The meaning of Jesus' declaration "This is my body" comes from the wealth of meaning in the Passover. The Lord intended to establish a new community of God. By commanding the Twelve "to do this in memory" of himself, he was making them the leaders of this new assembly ("church," i.e., *ekklesia*, which means "assembly") and was providing food for the future Church. It was not just any food. He gave not only a supper; he gave himself as food in the supper.

JESUS' DESIRE, OUR DESTINY

No wonder the early Church quickly began to call this meal the Eucharist. There is so much for which to be thankful. By his explicit action, Jesus connected us—through this meal—to his sacrificial death, a death that takes away our sin (John 1:29). By his own words, Jesus conveys to us—in some mysterious way—his own life, a life that he received from the heavenly Father (John 5:26). By his own design, Jesus unites us—through this meal—to himself and to all other believers throughout the world. The Eucharist gives us our identity as the children of God. The Eucharist is the source and summit of our Christian lives. In short, we are a eucharistic people.

Although this truth has been known since the very beginning of the Church, our understanding of it has deepened over time. This is known as the development of doctrine: the Holy Spirit guiding us to comprehend more and more about the truth God has revealed. Over those centuries, great saints and theologians have never ceased to marvel at the beauty and power of this sacrament of love. As St. Thomas Aquinas put it:

"Here is the Eucharist! What more do you want?"

When Pope John XXIII canonized St. Peter Julian Eymard in 1962, he called him "the great friend of the Eucharist." Born in 1811 near Grenoble, France, Eymard went on to become a priest of that diocese before joining the Marists. Later, he founded the Congregation of the Priests of the Blessed Sacrament, began an order of nuns called the Servants of the Blessed Sacrament, and established the Priests' Eucharistic League. Known for his deep love for our Lord in the Eucharist, he died in 1868.

Eymard was also a prolific writer. This is a small sample of his work:

The Eucharist is the noblest aspiration of our heart. Let us, therefore love it passionately! Some say: "But all this is exaggeration!" Love is nothing but exaggeration; to exaggerate is to go beyond the strict requirements of the law. Love must exaggerate.

All the love of the mortal life of the Savior, the love of a child in the crib, the love of zeal as the apostle of his Father in his preaching, the love of a victim on the cross—all these loves are gathered together, and triumphant in his heart, glorious and living in the Eucharist. That is where we should seek him and nourish ourselves with his love. He is also in heaven, but he is there for the angels and saints. He is in the Eucharist for us.

To believe in love is everything! It is not enough to believe in truth: One must believe in love—the love, that is, that our Lord Jesus Christ shows in the Blessed Sacrament. It is by living faith in the Eucharist that we return Christ's love for us. Pray for a simple and pure faith in the Eucharist. People may teach you the subtleties of its dogma, but Jesus alone can give you belief in it. Come and receive not only its consolation, but be strengthened in faith. Yes, here is the Eucharist! What more do you want?

In the end, no one can fully express the sweetness of this sacrament in which spiritual delight is tasted at its very source and in which we renew the memory of that surpassing love for us that Christ revealed in his Passion. It was to impress the vastness of his love more firmly upon the hearts of the faithful that our Lord instituted this sacrament at the Last Supper.[1]

2

THE REAL PRESENCE OF JESUS IN SCRIPTURE

JESUS HAS WRITTEN you a love letter. Through the inspiration of the Holy Spirit, he has shown you his love in the Bible. To best love him in return, it's important to pay careful attention to the words of Scripture regarding his expression of his love for us in the Eucharist.

The amazing truth is that our Lord's love shines forth not only in his wanting to share a meal with us but in actually giving himself to us *in* that meal. We call Christ in the Eucharist the Real Presence. That term means he gives himself completely: his body and blood, his soul and divinity.

DO THIS IN MEMORY OF ME

There is a phrase in the language of the Mass that is familiar but often misunderstood. After the priest consecrates the wine—that is, after it becomes the blood of Christ—but before he lifts the chalice, he repeats Jesus' words: "Do this in memory of me." That comes from two places in the New Testament that describe the institution of the Eucharist. The first is Luke's version of the Last Supper.

And he took bread, and when he had given thanks he broke it
and gave it to them, saying, "This is my body which is given
for you. Do this in remembrance of me." And likewise the cup
after supper, saying, "This cup which is poured out for you is
the new covenant in my blood (Luke 22:19–20).

The second is in Paul's first letter to the Corinthians (it is also the
only place in the New Testament outside the Gospels where the
words of institution can be found):

For I received from the Lord what I also delivered to you, that the
Lord Jesus on the night when he was betrayed took bread, and
when he had given thanks, he broke it and said, "This is my body
which is for you. Do this in remembrance of me." In the same way
also the cup, after supper, saying, "This cup is the new covenant
in my blood. Do this, as often as you drink it, in remembrance of
me." For as often as you eat this bread and drink the cup, you proclaim the Lord's death until he comes (1 Cor. 11:23–26).

It's highly likely that Paul's account was written first and that Luke
learned about this phrase from him. Today when we hear those
words, it is easy to assume that Jesus was commanding his original
Twelve to keep his memory before them (and that he was telling us
to do the same). At Mass, the words of the Eucharistic Prayer that
follow the consecration seem to add weight to this interpretation:

In memory of his death and resurrection,
We offer you, Father,
This life-giving bread and this saving cup.[2]
Father, calling to mind the death your Son endured for our
salvation,
his glorious resurrection
and ascension into heaven,
and ready to greet him when he comes again,
we offer you in thanksgiving
this holy and living sacrifice.[3]

Yes, this part of the Mass teaches us that we are supposed to recall Jesus' death and resurrection. But no, we are not supposed to limit the meaning of "do this in memory of me" to simply remembering. One reason such a narrow interpretation prevails is that the phrase has been torn from its immediate context in Corinthians and its wider biblical associations, too. But if we look at its place in biblical usage, it becomes easier to appreciate how much more it really means and how much more Jesus meant.

The word Paul used for "memory" or "remembrance" is the Greek word *anamnesis*. The phrase in which it occurs is always the same in the original Greek, even though it may be translated different ways. The same phrase, *eis ten emen anamnesin* (literally, "for my remembrance"), is found in both Corinthians and Luke. In Paul's writing, notice the word *for* begins verse 26 just after the phrase containing the term *anamensis*. Verse 26 explains the meaning of doing this in memory. It says that *anamnesis* involves a proclamation of the Lord's death in this act of consecration.

How does eating and drinking proclaim the Lord's death as verse 26 says? Proclaiming a message usually involves preaching, teaching, or speaking in some form, but, as we all know, actions speak louder than words. The eucharistic actions that Paul taught the Church in Corinth proclaim the Lord's death by making the Lord present to the worshiping community of faith. In other words, the Lord's death is present with the Church by the repetition of his words "this is my body."

Thus, *anamnesis* is more than mental recall of past events. It is an action that brings to the present place and time something from the past or from the other world.

In Greek culture, *anamnesis* could mean more of a process. As used by Plato, for example, the term denoted the movement of an abstract idea into this material world. It was one of his key concepts. For him, knowledge was an act of *anamnesis* or "remembering" whereby the realities of the world of forms (that is, ideas) came to people in this world. So *anamnesis* meant the means by which something in another world came to be embodied in this physical world. These meanings may have been in

Paul's mind as he used the term in the context of describing our Lord's original words.

Jesus' death—with all its forgiving power—now resides in heaven with him. *Anamnesis* brings that same reality to this world.

The Hebrew background of *anamnesis* is even more important. Even though Paul wrote in Greek, we must remember that he was a Jewish Pharisee (Phil. 3:5), and very possibly a rabbi (Acts 22:2) before his conversion to Christ on the road to Damascus (Acts 9:1–9). All this means that when he used *anamnesis*, he very possibly intended a Hebrew meaning as well as a Greek one.

We have discussed how important remembering was for the Jews as they celebrated the Passover. The Hebrew word for "memorial" is *zikaron*, and it has a connotation similar to *anamnesis* in Greek culture—more than mental recollection. The celebration of the Passover involved a participation in the original Exodus from Egypt. The purpose of this being an annual and perpetual event for the children of Israel was that every generation could experience the liberation from slavery that the generation in Egypt had experienced. Thus, *zikaron* connotes a participation in an event of the past rather than simply a mental recollection of that event.

What does this dual background mean? When Paul quotes Jesus as saying *eis ten emen anamnesin*, the apostle may understand the meaning both in Greek and Hebrew senses. One says that something in the heavenly world comes to this world and is present to those who worship. The other says that an event of the past is brought to the present through the celebration of the Eucharist. It's that combination that explains what the Church means by the term "Real Presence."

In the Eucharist, Jesus is truly present in his life, death, and resurrection. He is there not only in our minds but in our midst. He is there in reality. His death on the cross is an event of the past, but it also resides in heaven, where he is now seated at the right hand of the Father, because he took all his saving work into heaven (Heb. 4:14; 6:19–20; 7:26; 8:1). The Eucharist makes that past event and its heavenly reality present to those who participate in the Church's celebration. They are right *there*, at every Mass.

When Jesus commanded, "Do this *eis ten emen anamensin*," he wasn't saying simply "Don't forget me." He was telling his apostles to perform the same actions that he did in order to bring the reality of him back to this world.

Another New Testament reference to the Eucharist comes from Paul:

> The cup of blessing which we bless, is it not a participation in the blood of Christ? The bread which we break, is it not a participation in the body of Christ? Because there is one bread, we who are many are one body, for we all partake of the one bread (1 Cor. 10:16–17).

In the first verse, Paul asks two rhetorical questions to which he already knows the answers. He wants the Corinthians to see the true meaning of their Eucharist. It is a *real* participation in the body and blood of Christ. As that is the case, what must the cup and the bread *be* to make this participation in the blood and body of Christ possible? The most obvious and logical answer is that they

---

A Most Special Presence

The sacramental re-presentation of Christ's sacrifice, crowned by the Resurrection, in the Mass involves a most special presence that—in the words of Pope Paul VI:

> "is called 'real' not as a way of excluding all other types of presence as if they were 'not real,' but because it is a presence in the fullest sense: a substantial presence whereby Christ, the God-Man, is wholly and entirely present." This set forth once more the perennially valid teaching of the Council of Trent: The consecration of the bread and wine effects the change of the whole substance of the bread into the substance of the body of Christ our Lord, and of the whole substance of the wine into the substance of his blood. And the Holy Catholic Church has fittingly and properly called this change "transubstantiation."[2]

---

must *really be* the body and blood of Christ.

The second verse confirms this understanding. Paul says that partaking of the *one bread* makes many different people into *one body*. This is a kind of mystical unity that would be impossible if the bread and wine were not the true body and blood of Christ. Ordinary bread and wine simply cannot unite people into the body of Christ, but bread and wine transformed into Christ himself can. Paul was teaching that the Eucharist has the Real Presence of Christ's humanity within it.

To reiterate a central point: The Passover celebrated the redemption of God's people. When Jesus instituted the Eucharist at the Passover, he wanted us to know that the Eucharist is a salvation meal. This celebration, however, surpasses the Old Testament Passover because the new bread and wine consist of what they signify. In fact, that's the definition of a sacrament. Our Lord teaches us this reality when he used the words "Do this in remembrance [or memory] of me."

In the first century or the twenty-first, the notion that Jesus could give himself under the appearances of bread and wine may seem absurd to most people. That is why one of the longest chapters in the New Testament is devoted to this truth.

JESUS SAYS HIS PRESENCE IS REAL: JOHN 6

Our initial look at Jesus' words recorded by Paul and Luke suggests that belief in the Real Presence is thoroughly biblical. This is an important point, because the Catholic Church fully affirms Scripture to be the word of God, worthy of our full trust and confidence. And the unbroken Tradition passed down through the history of the Church confirms that the Church has always believed in the Real Presence. However, there is more biblical witness with regard to this truth.

The sixth chapter of the Gospel of John is the most important classic passage on the Real Presence of Christ in the Eucharist. As one might expect, it is one that has been subjected to differing interpretations throughout the history of Christianity, and especially by those who do not believe in the Real Presence. Needless to say, it is a chapter that should be studied thoroughly.

First, one can make a surface survey. Notice that the chapter has an overall progression that moves from a physical miracle to the meaning of that miracle:

- Verses 1–15: The miracle of Jesus feeding the crowd of five thousand men.
- Verses 16–21: Jesus meeting the disciples on the lake.
- Verses 22–34: The encounter between Jesus and the crowds who followed him.
- Verses 35–59: Jesus' teaching about himself as the bread of life, which is the meaning of the feeding of the multitude.
- Verses 60–71: The reactions of the crowds to Jesus' teaching on the bread of life.

The superficial sequence of the chapter contains a progression at a deeper level that reveals the true meaning of the miracle of the feeding of the five thousand. This movement reflects the way John tells the events of Jesus' life. He always wants to lead the reader to a more profound level of understanding. Chapter 6 presents us with three main levels of meaning:

Level One: In the physical miracle itself (verses 1–15), Jesus gives food to the people but wants to lead them to something more than just physical nourishment. Already within the multiplication

---

Efficacious Signs of Grace

"The sacraments are efficacious signs of grace, instituted by Christ and entrusted to the Church, by which divine life is dispensed to us. The visible rites by which the sacraments are celebrated signify and make present the graces proper to each sacrament. They bear fruit in those who receive them with the required dispositions."[3]

of loaves there are indications that point toward a fuller meaning. We are told that a large crowd followed Jesus "because they saw the signs which he did on those who were diseased" (verse 2). Later, John comments that the people proclaimed Jesus as the expected prophet when they "saw the sign which he had done" (verse 14). John framed the physical miracle in terms of a "sign" because he wanted us to see what that sign indicates.

Another clue to the deeper meaning is the use of the phrase "had given thanks" (verse 11). John chose the verb *eucharisteo* even though other synonyms were available (for example, *eulogeo*). The verb *eucharisteo* would have evoked the term *eucharistia* for the first readers of the Gospel and suggested to them that this miracle of multiplication is related to their practice of the Eucharist. The use of the word for "sign" and the verb *eucharisteo* to describe Jesus' action are pointers to the second level of meaning.

So, what is the meaning of the sign?

Level Two: A sign in John's Gospel means a miracle that points to Jesus as the unique bringer of God's gifts. For example, Jesus converted the water into wine in John 2 to show that he brings joy in abundance. We are told that this was his first sign in Cana of Galilee (John 2:11). In the second sign, Jesus brings healing to the sick (John 4:43–54). What is the meaning of the sign-miracle of Jesus feeding the multitudes? Jesus is the bread of life. Jesus (and John) challenge the reader to understand that divine life comes from him being the true bread from heaven (John 6:22–40). We can grasp the connection between the sign-miracle and the bread of life when John reminds us that Jesus spoke "near the place where they ate the bread after the Lord had given thanks" (verse 23). The verb *eucharisteo* is used again for "giving thanks," once more evoking a connection between the Eucharist and the feeding of the multitudes.

Even more importantly, Jesus challenges the Jews in a dialogue (verses 24–40) about where the true bread from heaven can be found. Jesus contrasts the true heavenly bread with the manna in the wilderness (verses 30–33). The manna only foreshadowed the bread that gives true life. Jesus explicitly identifies himself as the living bread: "I am the bread of life; he who comes to me shall not hunger, and he who believes in me shall never thirst" (verse 35). What is it about Jesus that makes him the bread of life? That question leads to the third and most profound level of meaning.

Level Three: It is set up by two key verbs. "The Jews then *murmured* at him" (verse 41) and "The Jews then disputed [*machomai*] among themselves" (verse 52). These verbs are important because they show that the dialogue in this latter part of the chapter proceeds by way of conflict.

By reading the first section in verses 41–51, we see that those present cannot believe in Jesus as "the bread which came from heaven" because they know him only as a man of their previous acquaintance (verse 42). Just as they fail to see anything more in the sign-miracle than a physical feeding, so also they fail to see anything more in Jesus than an everyday Jewish man. The climax of this dispute is when Jesus says, "I am the living bread which came down from heaven; if any one eats of this bread, he will live for ever; and the bread which I shall give for the life of the world is my flesh" (verse 51). In the progression of the chapter it is evident that Jesus, being the bread of life, is more than pure symbol or metaphor. The heavenly bread is his flesh. It is through his flesh that Jesus gives more than ordinary earthly life. He offers eternal life.

In these three levels of meaning, Jesus moves from the difficult to the impossible. Not only is he more than a man, but his flesh is more than ordinary human flesh. It gives eternal life. This leads to the last section of the chapter in which Jesus drives home his point even more strongly. It commences with the people asking, "How can this man give us his flesh to eat?" (verse 52).

Our Good Shepherd

"The good shepherd gave his life for the sheep that he may change his body and blood in our sacrament and that he may fill those sheep whom he had redeemed with the nourishment of his flesh."[4]

This is not only a logical question; it is the central question of Jesus' teaching in this chapter. Jesus affirms in the strongest possible terms the necessity of eating his flesh and drinking his blood:

> Truly, truly, I say to you, unless you eat the flesh of the Son of man and drink his blood, you have no life in you; he who eats my flesh and drinks my blood has eternal life, and I will raise him up at the last day. For my flesh is food indeed, and my blood is drink indeed (verses 53–55).

Everything in chapter six has led up to this moment—the punch line, as it were. This chapter bears careful analysis because people are often confused by the words of Jesus. Does he really mean to say that we must eat his flesh and drink his blood? Isn't that cannibalism? How can this be literally true?

The Church is certain that Jesus would not have gone on and on about eating his flesh and drinking his blood if all he meant to say was that we must believe in him. In other words, the Church doesn't reduce Jesus' words to simple belief. It insists that we must truly feed upon him as the sustenance of our lives.

The debate over whether to read Jesus' words as merely figurative obscures the more important question—the real question: Should his words about eating and drinking be reduced solely to belief in him, or should it be understood that belief in him comes to a climax in eating his flesh and drinking his blood?

The progression of the structure of John 6 points to Jesus as the bread of heaven whose flesh and blood communicate eternal life. The manna of the Old Testament was only symbolic of the real food from heaven that would come later. If that earlier symbol had to be eaten to sustain earthly life, how much more does the reality have to be eaten to sustain heavenly, eternal life? Without Christ's Real Presence, people cannot hope to enjoy eternal life with him. And without his sacred humanity (body and blood) there is no true Christ.

WHY IS THE REAL PRESENCE SO HARD TO BELIEVE?

The teaching on the Real Presence of Christ in the Eucharist is hard to believe. It defies comprehension. This fact shows itself clearly in the history of the Church, for there have been many occasions when people have doubted it. This should not be a surprise; it was hard for the people of Jesus' day to believe ["This is a hard saying; who can listen to it?" (John 6:60)]. The idea that human flesh could communicate eternal life from God in heaven seemed absurd to the Jews of Jesus' day, just as it does to many people today. That shows only human limitations—a persistent tendency to either make God too much like ordinary people or banish him into the realm of the completely spiritual.

The startling message of Scripture is that God became fully man while never ceasing to be God. John is the master of this truth when he writes, "The Word became flesh and dwelt among us, full of grace and truth" (John 1:14). This incarnation is also absurd from a purely human standpoint, but it, too, is the central tenet of Christian faith. God became man to accomplish salvation, and belief in his divine humanity is a requisite to being saved. That God-man gives himself to people under the appearances of bread and wine, and he says that they must partake of his divine humanity if they are to have eternal life.

The love that motivated God the Father to send his Son into the world as a man is the same love that motivates God the Son to lay down his life for his sheep (John 10:14–15) and to give himself as nourishment. This is a love that defies human understanding.

3

THE TRANSFORMING
MIRACLE OF
THE EUCHARIST

THERE IS A natural human tendency to think the only things that are real are those that can be seen, heard, touched, smelled, or tasted. But considered even for a moment, it is clear there are many realities the five senses are unable to detect.

Take love and affection. Signs of them can be seen, but neither can be seen directly. They are forever withheld from the senses. The Real Presence of Jesus is much like those intangible realities. The body and blood of Christ in the Eucharist cannot be seen, heard, touched, smelled, or tasted, but it is as real as the world the senses can experience. In the Blessed Sacrament, the Lord remains hidden under the appearances of bread and wine.

The witness of Scripture and the earliest Fathers testify to the faith of the Church in its belief in Jesus' Real Presence. At one level, this is enough to foster others' faith. The Bible is the inspired word of God; the united witness of the ancient Fathers points to the truths of the faith that every Catholic should hold. Still, it is only natural to ask questions. How can this amazing reality of Christ's presence be true? Can nothing more be said than "It's a miracle"? Is that the end of discussion? Fortunately, over the centuries the Church has asked these questions—and more—and has provided answers that are both satisfying and awe-inspiring.

THE REAL PRESENCE OF CHRIST IN EARLY CHRISTIANITY

Three early Church Fathers from the second to the fourth century provide great witness to the Church's belief in the Real Presence of Christ in the Eucharist:

1. St. Ignatius of Antioch
2. St. Justin Martyr
3. St. Cyril of Jerusalem

In his seven extant letters to the churches of Asia Minor, Ignatius provides us with some of the earliest texts that clearly show faith in the Real Presence. Ignatius was martyred in Rome sometime before 117 and, as the bishop of Antioch, may have known some of the apostles themselves. His testimony holds a lot of weight as we try to figure out what the early Church believed.

Like Paul expresses in 1 Corinthians, Ignatius is very concerned about threats to the unity of the Church. His worry is also reflected in the early Christian view of the sacrament. Just as there is a real authority of the bishop that derives from God, so there is a real connection between unity and the Eucharist. Ignatius says:

> Therefore, be diligent to employ only one Eucharist. For there is only one flesh of our Lord Jesus Christ, and there is only one cup for unity in his blood. There is one altar as there is one bishop together with the presbytery and the deacons, my fellow servants. The purpose of all this is so that your practices will be in accord with God's intention.[4]

Like his emphasis on the unity of the Church, Ignatius urges the importance of unity in the partaking of the Eucharist. "To employ only one Eucharist" means that a valid sacrament is one that comes from the authority of the bishop in union with Christ. The explanation for this validity lies in the reality that is present in the sacrament: "For there is only one flesh of our Lord Jesus Christ, and there is only one cup for unity in his blood."

The second witness from the Eastern (Greek-speaking) side of the Church is Justin Martyr. A convert from paganism, Justin remained a lay apologist his entire adult life and became known as a great defender of the faith. His knowledge of philosophy afforded him the background he needed to show the pagans of his day the reasonableness of Christianity. Justin's *First Apology* tries to convince readers that Christian belief in the Eucharist is not as absurd as it sounds to outsiders. The sequence of events in the liturgy[5] forms the background for his statements about the true meaning of this meal:

> This nourishment is called the Eucharist among us. No one is allowed to partake of it other than the one who believes the things taught by us to be true and the one whose sins are washed away and who received the washing leading to new birth. In this way it is for the one who lives as Christ handed down to us. For we do not receive these as common bread or as common drink. Rather, in the manner that Jesus Christ our Savior, who was made flesh through the word of God, took on [*sarx*] flesh and blood for our salvation, so too we are taught that the food, which is made the Eucharist by the prayer of the word from him, is in fact the flesh

---

The Bishop's Authority

"All of you follow your bishop, as Jesus Christ does the Father. Follow, too, the presbytery [the body of priests] as apostles and honor the deacons as the ordinance of God. Let no one practice anything having to do with the Church apart from the bishop. Let that Eucharist be considered valid which is under the authority of a bishop or under one he has appointed. Where the bishop appears, let the fullness [of the people] be there as the Catholic Church is there when Jesus Christ is. It is not permitted to baptize or to hold an agape feast apart from the bishop. Rather, whatever that one approves is acceptable to God that everything you do may be safe and valid."[5]

---

and blood of that Jesus who was made flesh. This food nourishes our blood and flesh by way of a transformation [*kata metabolen*]. The apostles in those memoirs by them called Gospels handed on in this way the things they were commanded, namely, that Jesus took bread, gave thanks [Eucharist] and said, "Do this in remembrance of me. This is my body." And taking the cup similarly, he gave thanks and said, "This is my blood."Give a share to them only. You know this or can learn it.[6]

Justin's realism comes through in his parallel between the Incarnation and the Eucharist. The presence of Christ's physical body is just as real in the Eucharist as it was in the womb of the Virgin Mary. The Eucharist "is in fact the flesh and blood of that Jesus who was made flesh."

Both Justin and Ignatius, then, testify to the faith of the second-century Church in showing their view of the sacrament: The Eucharist is nothing less than the true flesh of Jesus Christ. It's clear that this was a problematic teaching for the non-Christians of that time, but the Church could not soften or deny this Real Presence or without betraying itself.

In the the fourth century the third Eastern Father we are citing, Cyril of Jerusalem, expresses an awareness that one must not judge the Eucharist according to appearances:

Do not think of the bread and wine as mere bread and wine, for they constitute the body and blood of Christ by the Lord's own declaration. For even if your sense experience suggests this to you, let your faith rather confirm it for you. Do not judge the matter from taste. Rather, from your faith become fully persuaded without doubting, because you have been made worthy of the body and blood of Christ.[7]

Cyril's statements are important because they show that a distinction must be made between the appearances of bread and wine and the underlying reality of Christ's body and blood. Some Christians make the mistake of thinking that transubstantiation was an invention of medieval theologians without any basis in Scripture and ancient Christian faith. Such an idea is often cited as a compelling reason to reject the Church's teaching on this point. Part of the reason for this rejection is ignorance of the actual history behind this dogma. Cyril, as do many Western Fathers, show abundant evidence of a need for the Church to distinguish between appearance and reality when treating this profound mystery.

These three Church Fathers from the second to the fourth centuries are only the tip. Many more witness to the same fact: The early Church uniformly believed the Eucharist, properly consecrated and observed, to be the true and real presence of Jesus Christ, the incarnate God.

THE EPICLESIS: INVOCATION OF THE HOLY SPIRIT

The early Church Fathers' belief in the fact of the Real Presence does not answer how this presence comes to be. In general, when we ask how something was done, we sometimes want to know *who* did it; that is, we want to know *who* accomplished that particular

---

What Appears as Bread Is Not Bread

"Once you have learned these things, be fully assured that what appears as bread is not bread, even if your sense of taste says so. Rather, it is the body of Christ. And what appears to be wine is not wine even though your taste tells you it is. Rather, it is the blood of Christ. Concerning this David the Psalmist said, 'bread strengthens man's heart to gladden his face with oil.' Strengthen your heart because you partake of it as something spiritual. Gladden the face of your soul. Let that which is unveiled make you as one who has a pure conscience, beholding [or reflecting] the glory of the Lord. Move from glory to glory in our Lord Christ Jesus, to whom be honor, power, and glory forever and ever. Amen."[6]

---

act. When viewed in that context, a fuller appreciation of some of the answers to the "how" of the Real Presence can be found in the language of the liturgy. The eucharistic prayers of the Church help the people better understand what is known as the *Epiclesis*.

Epiclesis is a Greek noun meaning "the calling upon." It is used in Catholic liturgy to describe the moment when the Holy Spirit is invoked to descend on the gifts of bread and wine prior to the Words of Institution. (In some of the Eastern-rite churches it is thought that the *Epiclesis* is the moment when transubstantiation occurs and the body, blood, soul, and divinity of Christ become present in the hosts. This is not the standard discernment in the Latin-rite church, which is that transubstantiation happens at the Words of Institution.)

The invocation of the Holy Spirit in the *Epiclesis*—prior in the Mass to the Words of Institution—happens when the priest places his hands over the gifts and says:

> Let your Spirit come upon these gifts to make them holy
> so that they may become for us
> the body and blood of our Lord, Jesus Christ.[8]

The other three eucharistic prayers have similar language, all accompanied by the same gesture. For example, in the third prayer, the priest says:

> So, Father, we bring you these gifts.
> We ask you to make them holy
> by the power of your Spirit,
> that they may become the body and blood
> of your Son, our Lord Jesus Christ
> at whose command we celebrate this Eucharist.[9]

The prayers express the humble pleas of God's servants, both clergy and lay faithful, for God to bring his holy presence into this world to transform natural food into supernatural nourishment.

The work of the Holy Spirit is real. The hand gesture of the priest is only symbolic. The priest's hands don't accomplish anything. It is similar to the act of the priest's washing his hands in the Mass. As he does this, he prays silently or softly, "Lord, wash away my iniquity and cleanse me from my sin." The water doesn't cleanse him; it only symbolizes his prayer for forgiveness so the people see that he, too, is a sinner. It is essential to remember, however, that God has promised that if the rite is performed properly, he will make his Son present on the altar. That's why the Church says that the sacraments work *ex opere operato*, Latin for "by the work done." Thus the sacraments—including the eucharistic transformation— are effective by means of the sacramental rite itself and not because of the worthiness of the celebrant or participant.

In the *Epiclesis*, words and gestures combine to show the invisible presence of God the Spirit, much as the Spirit did in the Annunciation when he overshadowed the Virgin Mary to bring the Son of God in human flesh (Luke 1:35). In a sense the Eucharist continues the Incarnation of the Son of God so we may have life in him. The presence of the Holy Spirit, the third person of the Trinity, brings Jesus again to the Church.

But the more we have answers to this mystery, the more questions it raises. Even if we believe with Christians of all ages that the Holy Spirit possesses infinite power and can do all things, it still seems incomprehensible how bread can become a human body and wine can become human blood. If we feel baffled by this, we are in good company. The greatest theologians of the past have had the same reaction. That's why it is so important to understand transubstantiation.

Transubstantiation: The Transforming Miracle

We must remember that the Eucharist is a reality beyond normal human understanding, just as is the Incarnation. When John says, "The Word became flesh and dwelt among us" (John 1:14), we should be shocked at the audacity of such a claim. After twenty centuries of celebrating the birth of Christ, it is possible that we have become dulled to the original impact of this fact. In a similar way, the the celebration of the Eucharist can weaken our amazement at how incredible it should seem to the human mind to believe that this simple bread and wine can—and do—become the true body and blood of Christ. Unless we had it on the authority of God speaking through his Church, we should have never given credence to this dogma.

This ambivalence and wonder touched the medieval theologians when they spoke about transubstantiation. They knew they were between a rock and a hard place. On the one side, they were aware they would never be able to express the awe and majesty of this sacramental reality. On the other, they wanted to give the faithful some way of comprehending how the elements of bread and wine become Christ himself.

What, then, is transubstantiation? It is the transformation or conversion of the substance of the bread and wine into the substance of the body and blood of Christ. The word *substance* is important. A substance cannot be seen or touched, but it is very real. A substance is what underlies all the appearances we see. It is the thing in which those appearances cohere. Our bodies, for example, have many parts—in fact, millions upon millions of cells. But what makes all these parts work together? Most people today would say our brains. That is true. But what makes the brain work so well to coordinate these millions of body parts? The neurosciences have yet to reveal anything that makes it all hang together. In spite of all the physical explorations there is still something beyond the individual parts of our bodies. This "something extra" is the substance or essence of who we are.

In the terminology of medieval theology, what we can see and touch is called an accident or accidents—the outward appearances of things—but the substance is the invisible reality that binds all the appearances together. For example, I have ten fingers. If I happen to lose one of my fingers, my accident would change, but my substance—the essence of who I am—would not. In the normal course of nature, accidents change but substances do not.

In a way, transubstantiation is the opposite of what happens in nature. It is a change in the substance of bread and wine while leaving the accidents or appearances intact. The new substance is the body and blood of Christ while the appearances of the bread and wine (size or amount, texture, color, and so on) remain as they were. When we say that the consecrated bread and wine is the body and blood of Christ, we mean that the essence of Christ's humanity is under the appearances of bread and wine. And because Jesus Christ is *one* person in *two* natures (human and divine), all that he is comes with him. His divinity as well as his humanity come into the Eucharist and are communicated to all who receive him. Christ becomes *fully* present. He is there completely in this wonderful sacrament.

This is an incredible belief. It should not surprise us that people find it difficult to believe, especially those who have never spent much time examining a theology teaching or looked with any depth into a particular subject. Still, transubstantiation is a dogma of the highest order. It can never be relinquished or downplayed. It

---

"This Grace Grows in Those Who Receive Worthily"

"The form of this sacrament is the words of our Savior, by which he brings about [*conficere*] this sacrament. For the priest who speaks in the person of Christ brings about this sacrament. For by the power of the words themselves the substance of the bread is changed into the body of Christ and the substance of the wine into the blood. Yet, this happens in such a way that the whole Christ is contained under the species [elements] of bread and the whole Christ is under the species of wine. The whole Christ is also under each part of the consecrated host and the consecrated wine after the separation. The effect of this sacrament for those who partake worthily is the union of human beings with Christ. Because a man is incorporated into Christ through grace and united to his members, it follows that through this sacrament grace grows in those who receive worthily. And every effect that material food and drink yields for bodily life—sustaining, growing, healing, delighting—this sacrament works as it were for spiritual life."[7]

---

is essential for a Catholic to believe, so essential that not believing it puts into serious question a person's understanding of the faith. But how do we *know* it is true?

In several ways.   1 - historical witness

Transubstantiation has been the uniform teaching of the Church. This is important because sometimes people think that medieval theologians simply concocted the idea. Such a complicated teaching, some critics say, was not part of the time-honored teaching of the Church. Let's clarify this point. It is true that the word *transubstantiation* does not appear in Church documents until about the tenth century, but the idea has been there a much longer time. In the second century, Justin Martyr spoke of the body of Christ being in the sacrament "by way of transformation," and Cyril of Jerusalem clearly distinguished between appearances and reality. These statements are the background for transubstantiation. Even more explicitly, St. Ambrose in the fourth century wrote about the change of the elements:

> We see that grace can accomplish more than nature, yet so far we have been considering instances of what grace can do through a prophet's blessing. If a human blessing had power even to change nature, what do we say of the divine consecration itself, in which the very words of the Lord and Savior are at work? For the sacrament that you receive is brought about by the word of Christ. If the words of Elijah had power even to bring down fire from heaven, will not the words of Christ have power to change the natures of the elements? You have read that in the creation of the whole world he spoke and they came to be; he commanded and they were created. If Christ could by speaking create out of nothing what did not yet exist, is he not able to change existing things into something they previously were not? It is no lesser feat to create new natures for things than to change their existing natures.[10]

The parallels that Ambrose draws between the creation of the world, Elijah, and the Eucharist demonstrate how completely he believed in the transformation of the sacramental species. He did not use the term *transubstantiation*, but he obviously expressed the idea behind it. The Church believed in the truth contained in the term *transubstantiation* long before it ever used that particular word to express it.   *2 official dogmatic declaration*

Second, the notion of a miraculous change endured for centuries before being challenged by a series of controversies from the eighth to the eleventh centuries. These disputes eventually evoked an official definition of the dogma. It was first declared at the Fourth Lateran Council in 1215, reaffirmed by the Council of Florence (1438–45), and developed by the Council of Trent in the sixteenth century in response to Protestant denials of its truth. Trent expressed it succinctly and clearly:

> Christ our Redeemer, who offered us his body under the species of bread, said that it was true. And so it has always been the persuasion of God's Church, and therefore this synod declares that through the consecration of bread and wine there takes place (*fieri*) a conversion of the whole substance of bread into the substance of the body of Christ our Lord and of the whole substance of the wine into the substance of his blood. This conversion has been conveniently and appropriately called transubstantiation by the Holy Catholic Church.[11]

This decree shows that both the Real Presence and transubstantiation enjoy the highest status of dogma within the Church. They are defined as *de fide* truths that all Catholics must believe.

The third reason to believe is far more important than historical witness and official dogmatic declaration. In fact, ultimately, those two depend on the third, which is this: Jesus Christ said it. He is God in the flesh, and he has all the authority of his Father in heaven (Matt. 11:28; 28:18). Some may consider this simplistic, but what could be more reasonable than to believe someone who is all-knowing and all-powerful?

 3X said

Consider the character of the one who spoke the words "This is my body." The meaning of the words of consecration cannot be separated from the person who first spoke them. If Jesus were only a man, then perhaps he meant only to compare two things—his body and the bread—as if to say, "Think of this bread as my body." If he was acting only as a man, perhaps all he meant was to treat the bread as a mere symbol of his body. But Jesus Christ is more than a man. He is the unique God-Man possessing in himself the fullness of divinity and humanity. This fact makes the speaking of these words potentially different from the same words spoken by one who is solely human. Being fully God, Jesus Christ has the power to use words in a performative rather than simply a descriptive or metaphorical manner. A performative use of language means that the words *perform* the action that they *signify*. Ordinary humans typically use words only to describe things as when somebody says, "This house is green," or to point to things, such as "This is my house." Sometimes human beings describe things through comparisons, such as "My house is a castle." Human beings cannot perform actions by their words except under carefully selected circumstances. In a court of law, a judge may declare the case closed. His words close the case. Or in a special ceremony a government official may say, "I dub this ship . . ." and then give the ship a name. These cases are special and limited.

Not so with God. Of course, God can use words as human beings do, but he can also perform the actions signified by the words he uses. This use is most clearly seen in the first chapter in the Bible. Genesis 1 tells us that God said, "Let there be light" and "Let there be a firmament" and "Let the waters under the heavens be gathered together." Genesis intends to teach us not that God is describing things but that he is bringing them about. These words accomplish what they say. They perform the act they describe.

When Jesus said, "This is my body," was he describing something or making a comparison as ordinary human beings do? Or was Jesus performing an act when he made that statement? It is possible, of course, that the bare use of the words could be a description or a metaphor, but the reasons mentioned above lead us to think that he intended to perform an action by his words. It is more likely that Jesus intended to make that bread into his body during that first Passover celebration. As the God-Man, Jesus' words could change bread into his body, just as his words once changed water into wine (John 2:1–12).

To all appearances, Jesus does not say these words again. They are part of history. That would indeed be the case if Jesus were not alive today. But Jesus is alive and speaks the same words he spoke at that first Eucharist in the Upper Room. He uses the mouth of a properly ordained priest to convey his power of transforming the bread and wine into his own substance. This is why the priest must say not "This is *his* body" but "This is *my* body."

The Real Presence of Jesus in the Eucharist comes about through transubstantiation. The material gifts of bread and wine are brought to him. By the union of the invisible power of the Holy Spirit coming at the *Epiclesis* with the audible words that the living Jesus pronounces through the voice of the priest at the consecration, Jesus transforms our gifts of bread and wine into his sacred humanity (his body, blood, soul, and divinity). Through this union of the spiritual and the material, Jesus gives us himself in his supper of love.

Part Two

THE EUCHARIST
AS SACRIFICE

4

THE SACRIFICE THAT
TAKES AWAY OUR SIN

JESUS ONCE SAID to his apostles, "Greater love has no man than this, that a man lay down his life for his friends. You are my friends" (John 15:13–14). By his death on the cross, Jesus has shown us the full extent of his love for us. If we want to become better at loving God, we need to understand the sacrificial nature of our Lord's love. That is one of the main reasons that the Catholic Church insists on seeing the Eucharist as a sacrifice. According to the Church's constant teaching, the Mass is a true sacrifice offered to God the Father that can take away sin. Unfortunately, the sacrificial reality of the Eucharist is not well understood today and has been undervalued in some circles. Yet participating in the holy sacrifice of the Mass is one of the greatest privileges afforded to us as human beings.

THE EUCHARISTIC SACRIFICE IS THE CHURCH'S CONSTANT TEACHING

As noted, early Church Fathers uniformly affirmed the Real Presence of Christ's body and blood. Those writings also taught that the Eucharist is a true sacrifice to God. The *Didache*—written in the first century and rediscovered in 1875 in a library in Istanbul, Turkey—confirms what the Church had always thought, namely, that the Real Presence was the uniform belief of ancient Christianity. As one of the earliest Christian documents outside the New Testament, the *Didache* also speaks of the Eucharist as a sacrifice:

> On the Lord's day, once you have gathered, break the bread of the Lord, and hold Eucharist, confess your transgressions that your sacrifice may be pure. Let not anyone who has a quarrel with his friend join you until they reconcile that your sacrifice not be defiled. This is what was spoken by the Lord, "In every place and time offer to me a pure sacrifice because I am a great king, says the Lord, and my name is marvelous among the Gentiles" (Mal 1:11).[12]

This passage shows that during the last half of the first century (or at the latest the first quarter of the second) the worship of the Church was conceived in sacrificial terms. While this text does not tell us what kind of sacrifice (for example, a thank-offering or one offered for expiation) was intended, it does emphasize two features: The worshipers must be pure in offering their sacrifice, and the Church viewed the Eucharist as a fulfillment of Old Testament prophecy. Implicit in these two teachings was the idea that the worshipers offer themselves to God through the Eucharist.

This line of thinking appears in a writing of second-century witness Justin Martyr. He insists that the Eucharist is also a fulfillment of Old Testament types (or signs) and prophecy:

> The offering of finest wheat, I say, O gentlemen, which was passed down to be offered for those who had been cleansed from leprosy, was a type [or sign] of the bread of the Eucharist. Jesus Christ our Lord passed this down to be done in remembrance of his Passion, in which he suffered to cleanse the souls of men from all evil. He wanted us to give thanks [*eucharistein*] for the creation of the world and all it contains as well as for his

liberating us from the evil that we have done and for having destroyed the powers and authorities in a perfect destruction with the passion that was in his will. Therefore, God speaks about those sacrifices that were at one time offered by you all, as I said, through Malachi, one of the twelve prophets, "My will is not among you," says the Lord, "and I will not accept the sacrifices from your hands. Therefore, from the rising of the sun to its setting my name is glorified among the Gentiles, and in every place incense and a pure offering is offered to my name because my name is great among the nations," says the Lord, "but you defile it" (Mal. 1:11). Now he speaks beforehand about the sacrifices offered by us Gentiles in every place—that is, the bread of the Eucharist and similarly the cup of the Eucharist—when he says that we "glorify his name, but you defile it."[13]

In the quotation from Malachi 1:11, he does not appear to be juxtaposing the Eucharist as a *true* sacrifice as opposed to the Jewish ones. Rather he seems to be portraying the Eucharist as the *fulfillment* of what the Old Testament sacrifices were meant to be. Justin implies the universality (catholicity) of the Church when he speaks of "the sacrifices offered by us Gentiles in every place." He sees that the truth of Malachi's words can be fulfilled only in a religion that covers the earth. We have no reason to believe that Justin knew of the *Didache*, and yet both quote Malachi 1:11 to prove that the Christian sacrifice of the Eucharist is what the prophet intended. Many, if not all, early Christian communities had learned the prophet's words and applied them to their own worship. This suggests a uniformity of belief among the earliest Catholic communities.

This impression of uniformity grows even stronger when we look at St. Irenaeus, who was the bishop of Lyons (in ancient Gaul, now France) in the second half of the second century (c. 150–180). Irenaeus had grown up in the Eastern, Greek-speaking part of the Church. As he tells us elsewhere, when he was a boy he had heard Polycarp, the venerated bishop of Smyrna (in Asia Minor). Having moved to the Western, Latin-speaking part of the Church, Irenaeus became one of the foremost defenders of the faith against Gnosticism, the heresy that holds that salvation is by knowledge and possessed by only a few. In his renowned *Against Heresies*, he speaks of the Eucharist as an offering to God:

> But he [Christ] also counseled his disciples to offer the first fruits of his creatures to God, not as if God needed anything, but that they [the people] might not be unfruitful or ungrateful. That which was bread from the creation he took, gave thanks [*eucharistein*], saying, "This is my body." And similarly, the cup from the creature he professed to be his own blood and taught that it is the new offering [*oblatio*] of the new covenant. It is this offering that the Church has received from the apostles and that it offers to God throughout the world. It is offered to God, who gives us nourishment, that is, the first fruits of his own gifts in the new covenant.[14]

In the face of Gnostic claims to possess the true form of Christianity, Irenaeus argues that this offering of the Eucharist descends from the apostles themselves. Like earlier authors, he also alludes to Malachi 1:11 to stress that the offering of bread and wine is a pure oblation or sacrifice to God.

About a century later, we hear a fourth witness to the eucharistic sacrifice from yet another geographical region of the Church. St. Cyprian was the bishop of Carthage (in northern Africa) in the mid-third century. In one of his letters, he draws a clear line from the priesthood of Christ through the ministerial priesthood to the Eucharist:

> If Christ Jesus, our Lord and God, is himself a high priest of God the Father, and offered himself as a sacrifice to the Father, and commanded that this be done in commemoration of him, certainly that priest truly acts by the power of Christ who imitates what Christ did and offers a true and full sacrifice in the church to God the Father if indeed he begins by offering what Christ himself appears to have offered.[15]

Cyprian makes explicit what was implicit before. The sacrifice of the Church comes from Christ's priesthood because the human priest is the instrument of Christ to offer exactly what the Redeemer himself offered. Because the Eucharist is the offering of Christ to the Father, it is "a true and full sacrifice in the church to God the Father."

More than a millennium later, when this teaching was challenged during the Protestant Reformation, the bishops at the Council of Trent knew that they were obliged to reassert the sacrificial nature of the Mass:

> Christ instituted the new Passover that he might be offered up by the Church under visible signs through the ministry of priests in memory of his exit from this world to the Father. He did this when he redeemed us by the shedding of his own blood and when he rescued us from the power of darkness and transferred us into his own kingdom. And this is in fact the pure offering [*oblatio*] that cannot be defiled by any unworthiness or malice of those who offer it. The Lord spoke ahead of time about his own name when he said through Malachi that it would be great among the Gentiles "as a pure offering in every place" (Mal. 1:11). The apostle Paul was not obscure when he wrote to the Corinthians that those who are defiled by communion in the table of demons cannot also be partakers of the Lord's table understanding by *table* an altar in both cases.[16]

Since the Council of Trent, the Church has always emphasized that the sacrifice of the Mass must be understood as a *de fide* teaching, because to deny it would fly in the face of the united witness of the Church throughout the ages. This is why the Second Vatican Council also reasserted this truth: "Taking part in the eucharistic sacrifice [is] the source and summit of the Christian life."[17]

In his sustained attempt to promote the teachings of Vatican II, Pope John Paul II emphasized the importance of this dogma for the Church today. In 2003, he wrote:

Truly, in the Eucharist he [Christ] shows us a love that goes all
the way "to the end" (John 13:1), a love that knows no limit.
The basis of universal love in the eucharistic sacrifice rests on
the very words of the Savior, for when he instituted it, he said
not only "This is my body," "this is my blood," but he added:
"which is given for you . . . poured out for you" (Luke 22:19).
Strictly speaking, Christ told them not only that he would give
them his body to eat and his blood to drink, but he also dis-
closed its sacrificial power because he made present his sacrifice
in a sacramental way. He was about to complete this sacrifice
in a few hours on the cross for the salvation of all. "The Mass
is at once and inseparably the sacrificial memorial in which the
sacrifice of the cross is perpetuated and also the sacred banquet
of communion in the body and blood of the Lord."[18]

Far from being of secondary importance for Catholics, the gift of
Christ's sacrifice in the Mass remains crucial for the life and health
of the Church. Why is this so central and in need of reemphasis?
The quotations from the Council of Trent and John Paul II clarify
the issue for us. The Eucharist makes present to the Church today
the original sacrifice of Christ on the cross of Calvary. It is only
this sacrifice that—as Trent points out, referring to Paul's words
in Colossians 1:13—"delivered us from the dominion of darkness
and transferred us to the kingdom of his beloved Son."

The Father's love for his Son Jesus extends to us too as he offers us the same sacrifice of his Son in the Eucharist. We offer that
same sacrifice back to the Father with the plea that he would accept
us through his Son. We can be reconciled to God only through
Christ's sacrifice. For this reason, our worship today must contain
that same sacrifice if we are to continue to be acceptable to the
Father.

From the first century to the twenty-first, the Church has believed in the eucharistic sacrifice, not just a sacrifice of praise to
God in thanksgiving for Jesus. The sacrifice that occurs in the Mass
is nothing less than Jesus' sacrifice on the cross for us. This sacrifice
of Calvary *must be present* because the priest who offered the sacri-

fice and the sacrifice itself, the victim, are both present in the person of Jesus Christ. Since he really is present in the Mass, all that he is comes along as well. However, even though this teaching may be the constant faith of the Church, is it really in the Bible? Especially for those whose confidence in the Catholic Church is not high, can we provide biblical reasons for this sacrifice of the Mass?

Is this Teaching Biblical?

To answer this question, we need to study three teachings of the Bible:

1. Jesus' death on the cross as a sacrifice
2. Jesus' role as a priest in giving this self-offering
3. The extension of this sacrifice on the cross through space and time

From time immemorial people have desired to know the meaning of death. Christians are no different. When people think of the death of Jesus, they can easily view what happened from a natural perspective. From this standpoint, Jesus' death on the cross was a Roman crucifixion that meant nothing more than a punishment for his supposed crimes. But the New Testament has so much more to say than this bare historical fact. For the writers of the New Testament—and for us who follow their teachings as God's—the death of Jesus was the supreme sacrifice for the sins of the world. Understanding Christ's death as a sacrificial offering is crucial if we are to be aware of the meaning and the power of the Eucharist.

Paul puts it succinctly: "Walk in love, as Christ loved us and gave himself up for us, a fragrant offering and sacrifice to God" (Eph. 5:2). "Gave up," "fragrant offering" and "sacrifice" mark the unmistakable truth that Jesus' death acted as a sacrifice that pleased the Father. The same word for "offering," *prosphore*, is used in connection with Jesus' body in Hebrews 10:10: "And by that will [God's will] we have been sanctified through the *offering* of the body of Jesus Christ once for all." Two verses later the word *sacrifice* describes Jesus' death on the cross: "When Christ had offered for all time a single *sacrifice* for sins, he sat down at the right hand of God" (Heb. 10:12). Jesus' death is no mere human death; it had the meaning of a sacrifice.

Hebrews also tells us the purpose of Jesus' sacrificial death: "He [Christ] has appeared once for all at the end of the age to put away sin by the sacrifice of himself" (Heb. 9:26). Similar language in John 1:29 echoes this belief in the removal of sin: "Behold, the Lamb of God, who takes away the sin of the world!" These words, familiar from the Mass, embody the truth that our access to God in worship comes through the sacrificial death of Jesus. Also in Hebrews, the connection between Christ's death and our worship is brought out explicitly:

> Therefore, brethren, since we have confidence to enter the sanctuary by the blood of Jesus, by the new and living way which he opened for us through the curtain, that is, through his flesh, and since we have a great high priest over the house of God, let us draw near with a true heart in full assurance of faith (Heb. 10:19–22).

Jesus' flesh and blood, offered on the altar of the cross, opened heaven for us to enter into the very presence of God. All this is based on Jesus' own words when he said, "For the Son of Man also came not to be served but to serve, and to give his life as a ransom for many" (Mark 10:45). The term "ransom" (*lutron*) signals a payment for sin that liberates those for whom it is offered. Jesus' death was that payment for our sins because we ourselves could not pay it. His sacrifice on the cross, the offering of his perfect life and obedience, cleared the way for our entry into God's presence. This is what we experience in every Mass. Heaven opens because the sacrificial death of our Redeemer is there to present us as an acceptable sacrifice to God.

Many non-Catholic Christians do not understand the importance of viewing the Mass as a true sacrifice. In their minds, this belief detracts from the uniqueness of Christ's final sacrifice on the cross. They say that calling the Eucharist a sacrifice diminishes the power and significance of Jesus' death on the cross. The Church insists that other Christians should understand the Mass, and specifically the Eucharist, as a true sacrifice that takes away sin.

One of the most compelling reasons is already implicit in what we have said about the Real Presence of Christ in the Eucharist. If, as the Church teaches, the Eucharist is truly Jesus Christ, then all that Christ is comes with him. This includes his sacrificial death on the cross. Wherever Jesus Christ is, there is a sacrifice. It is not an additional sacrifice to what he did on the cross. It is the same sacrifice, newly presented.

The powerful message of the gospel is not only that Jesus died as a sacrificial victim but that he himself was the priest who offered that sacrifice. Here again, Hebrews plays a key role in our understanding.

Its author calls Jesus "a great high priest" (Heb. 4:14) and in the next chapter recounts the Jewish understanding of what a priest was to do. Jesus is called an eternal priest "after the order of Melchizedek" (Heb. 5:6; cf. 7:1–3). Throughout the remainder of the letter, the author contrasts Jesus' priesthood with the Levitical (that is, the Aaronic) priesthood to argue that Jesus' priesthood is far superior to that of the Old Covenant. To grasp what is being said, we need to remember that the recipients of this letter were Jewish Christians who were tempted to return to worship in the temple in Jerusalem and to abandon their faith in Christ (Heb. 2:1ff).

Hebrews says that perfection did not come through the normal Aaronic priesthood (Heb. 7:11) but that Jesus' priesthood is greater because it is based on a better, new covenant (Heb. 7:22; 8:7–13). Jesus' sacrifice holds eternal value that does not need repeating. "He has no need, like those high priests, to offer sacrifices daily, first for his own sins and then for those of the people; he did this once for all when he offered up himself" (Heb. 7:27).

This theme of Jesus as the priest who offers his own life as a sacrifice presages Mark 10:45, that Jesus came "to give his life as a ransom for many." In Hebrews 9:11ff, we hear the author explaining in what sense Jesus' offering is superior. His priesthood is exercised in the heavenly tabernacle (Heb. 9:11). His offering is not bulls and goats but his own blood. This sacrifice obtains eternal redemption (Heb. 9:12). That is why it can "purify your conscience from dead works to serve the living God" (Heb. 9:14).

From these texts, we can now understand why the Church views Jesus' offering of himself on the cross as a priestly act that took away the sins of humanity. This is an astounding truth, because in no other case are the priest and the sacrifice the same person. But this paradoxical situation is precisely the message of love. Jesus' love for sinners moves him to offer a sacrifice that takes away the sins of the world (John 1:29), and no sacrifice will accomplish this forgiveness except his own perfect life offered on the cross.

Many Christians still find it difficult to understand what Jesus' priesthood and sacrifice have to do with our worship. Even if they believe that their sins are forgiven by Christ's offering himself on the cross, they see this as a one-time event that gets applied to a person's heart when he believes in Jesus as Savior. Thus, worship for them is simply a response of thanksgiving for this perfect sacrifice.

Catholics hold this understanding as well, but they also see Jesus' sacrifice on the cross as extending through space and time. Earlier, several of the Fathers of the Church quoted Malachi 1:11 as a prophetic anticipation of the Eucharist. At the heart of this are the prophet's words, "For from the rising of the sun to its setting my name is great among the nations, and in every place incense is offered to my name, and a pure offering; for my name is great among the nations, says the Lord of hosts."

The Prince of Priests

"Christ is the prince of priests who offers his own blood for us. We priests follow him, as much as we can, to offer the sacrifice for the people. Even though we are very weak, yet it is an honorable sacrifice. . . . Christ himself can be seen as making the offering in us. His word sanctifies the sacrifice that is offered."[8]

This scriptural quote contains at least three significant points. The phrases "from the rising of the sun to its setting," "in every place," and "among the nations" suggest that the offering being talked about is going to be universal (catholic) and perpetual. This would have been quite strange from an Old Testament point of view, since only the Jews could offer to God an acceptable sacrifice in the temple in Jerusalem. The context of this verse (Mal. 1:7–12) indicates that God was displeased with Israel's sacrifices because those offerings were lacking. The answer God gives is to promise a new time and a new place where "a pure offering" will be given.

The geographical reference—"in every place"—shows that this new offering will be a universal sacrifice. The temporal description ("from the rising of the sun to its setting") indicates no time zone on earth will lack this sacrifice. It is continual and perpetual. Finally, the phrase "among the nations" (in Hebrew, *goyim*) can refer only to the Gentiles. But in the Old Covenant way of thinking, how can the Gentiles offer "a pure sacrifice" to God? Here is where the Church's early theologians spotted a description of the Eucharist, because it is nothing less than the pure lamb of God who takes away the sin of the world.

The Mass is our way to become connected to that one great sacrifice. Malachi 1:11 cannot be referring to Jesus' death directly because that sacrifice was not "from the rising of the sun to its setting" nor "in every place." But if the Eucharist contains Jesus Christ under the appearances of bread and wine, then it can fulfill the language of Malachi, because it is the only "pure offering" that is made everywhere, at all times, and especially "among the nations." We are reminded of this at Mass every time we pray:

> From age to age you gather a people to yourself
> so that from east to west
> a perfect offering may be made to the glory of your name.[19]

The English translation of this prayer now in use may obscure the reference to Malachi 1:11 by using "east to west" instead of "from the rising of the sun to its setting" and by using "perfect offering" instead of "pure offering." The original Latin clearly alludes to Malachi to show that the Church's faith in Christ's pure self-offering comes from the authority of Scripture itself.

The only way that the celebration of the Eucharist on earth can have this application through space and time is because every earthly Mass is in fact a reflection and embodiment of the one heavenly Mass where the pure sacrifice for our sins resides. Scripture brings this out with a beautiful description of Christian worship:

> But you have come to Mount Zion and to the city of the living God, the heavenly Jerusalem, and to innumerable angels in festal gathering, and to the assembly of the first-born who are enrolled in heaven, and to a judge who is God of all, and to the spirits of just men made perfect, and to Jesus, the mediator of a new covenant, and to the sprinkled blood that speaks more graciously than the blood of Abel. (Heb. 12:22–24).

The author contrasts Jewish worship (Heb. 12:18–22) with the worship of Christians by saying in essence that in every place where Christians celebrate the Lord's Passover meal, they are in fact worshiping in heaven. It is in heaven where there are "innumerable angels in festal gathering" and "the assembly of the first-born." It is in heaven where there is "a judge who is God of all" and where there are "the spirits of just men made perfect," that is, the saints. Most of all, it is in heaven where there is "Jesus, the mediator of a new covenant" and his "blood that speaks more graciously than the blood of Abel."

A truer and more beautiful description of the Mass could not be given. Every time we celebrate the holy sacrifice of the Eucharist, no matter how humble the surroundings, we are in touch with all these heavenly realities. Jesus and his sacrificial blood are there with us because we are in heaven and heaven is among us.

WHY IS THE EUCHARISTIC SACRIFICE SO IMPORTANT?

Most people realize that nothing good in life can be achieved without sacrifice. To reach an important goal, we must be willing to give up something else. Nothing could be truer than this when we think of the holy sacrifice of the Mass. Jesus wanted to reconcile us to God, and he could do that only by sacrificing his life for us. God is infinitely holy, and only an infinitely holy sacrifice would bring us back to God. So when Christ died on the cross, he satisfied the demands of justice. We are reconciled through his death. The ultimate good of our salvation has been achieved by the ultimate good of his death and resurrection.

The Eucharist extends that death and resurrection into our place and time. We are constantly reconnected with Jesus through the Mass. That celebration allows us to live constantly in the presence of God the Father through the presence of God the Son. His sacrifice on Calvary is reinserted into our lives through the liturgy of the Church. The Mass is nothing less.

Such a gift is beyond words. The only appropriate response is exactly what motivated Jesus to sacrifice his life in the first place: love. Love is why we must always keep the Eucharist as a sacrifice before our eyes. It proclaims the love of the Lamb of God and beckons us to love him as he first loved us.

"The Source and the Summit of the Whole Christian Life"

In giving his sacrifice to the Church, Christ has also made his own the spiritual sacrifice of the Church, which is called to offer itself in union with the sacrifice of Christ. This is the teaching of the Second Vatican Council concerning the faithful: "Taking part in the eucharistic sacrifice, which is the source and the summit of the whole Christian life, they offer the divine victim to God, and offer themselves along with it."[9]

Part Three

THE EUCHARIST
AS COMMUNION

5

WORTHY RECEPTION
OF THE EUCHARIST

FROM SCRIPTURE AND the constant historical witness of the Church, we learn that Jesus Christ is truly present in the Eucharist—present with his body, his blood, his human soul, and his divinity. With this fullness of his presence, Christ gives nothing less than his own sacrifice on Calvary. It is that sacrifice that takes away our sins. Now let's explore *how* the faithful Catholic receives Jesus in the Eucharist.

It may sound strange at first to ask how we should receive the Blessed Sacrament. After all, don't we just walk up to the front of the church and accept the consecrated host and wine? Or maybe such a question has to do with whether we should receive the consecrated host in the hand or on the tongue. In the post-Vatican II reform of the liturgy, the faithful are allowed to receive Communion either way. But the question of how to receive Communion really goes deeper than that. It has to do with the relationship between the outward act and the inner dispositions of the one receiving our Lord in the Eucharist.

Throughout history, the Church has based its approach to Holy Communion on the words of Paul in the New Testament and has taken the utmost care in helping God's people prepare for receiving the Eucharist. In the sixteenth century, the Council of Trent carefully explained how we should receive the sacrament and taught there are three ways to do that:

1. Spiritually and sacramentally
2. Spiritually only
3. Sacramentally only

It is best to receive the Eucharist both sacramentally and spiritually. This means that the communicant receives the sacred host and the precious blood into his mouth—that is, sacramentally—and also possesses the proper inner dispositions—that is, spiritually—so that he obtains the most benefit from this sacramental participation.

When this sacramental reception is not possible (as discussed later) the communicant may have some benefit through spiritual communion alone. To commune with Christ spiritually is to be united to him through the Holy Spirit, but this kind of communion does not bring us the true body and blood of Christ. Some benefits of Christ's death and resurrection may still be communicated to our souls during this spiritual act of communion.

The least desirable situation is to receive sacramentally alone. In this case, the communicant does receive the body and blood of Christ because Christ is present in the sacred species whether the person's heart is in the right place or not. But when a person receives Holy Communion without the proper dispositions of the heart, he is deprived of the benefits that would normally accrue to a person whose heart *is* properly disposed. Paul goes so far as to say such a person "eats and drinks judgment upon himself" (1 Cor. 11:29). This last possibility implies that preparing to receive Jesus in Holy Communion is not an act to be taken lightly.

PREPARING TO RECEIVE JESUS IN COMMUNION

There is no greater privilege on earth than receiving the true body and blood of Christ. The better we understand what this act means, the better we will be ready to receive our Lord with the greatest profit. Reception of the Eucharist involves nothing less than being intimately united with the true and living God in the depths of our souls, in those secret recesses of our hearts where our true selves reside. God wants to unite himself to us sinners who have turned away from him. He wants to not just forgive us but heal us of the wounds with which original sin has scarred our lives. That healing clears the way for us to be united with Christ in the most intimate manner possible: Christ's heart joined to our hearts as our bodies receive his body.

Given this rich understanding, it is no wonder that Paul warns us in his first letter to the Corinthians that we must pay careful attention to how we receive the sacrament. Chapter 11 of this epistle is unique in the New Testament because it explains how easily Christians can abuse the great privilege of receiving the Eucharist.

Paul brought up the subject of the Lord's Supper because of the abuses that had crept into the liturgy of the Corinthian church. In first-century Corinth, the eucharistic celebration had become an occasion for factionalism (1 Cor. 11:18) and for an air of superiority on the part of some (1 Cor. 11:20–22). These actions and attitudes denied the very meaning of the Eucharist, because the sacrament signifies unity as opposed to factionalism and brotherly love as opposed to self-importance. This, and more, led Paul to rebuke the Corinthians in the strongest terms possible, because they had not understood what the holy supper implied (1 Cor. 11:27–34).

The key word in this passage is "unworthy" (*anaksios*) in verse 27, a term that reverberates throughout the eucharistic prayers of the Church in later history. What does it mean to partake of the consecrated host and wine unworthily?

Paul never says specifically. Why? Because it would take too long to list all the specifics of what might constitute partaking in that manner. But the apostle does give some key phrases to help us understand. Verse 28 says, "Let a man examine himself, and so eat of the bread and drink of the cup." Then, in verse 29, he speaks of condemnation for the one "who eats and drinks without discerning the body." In verse 31, he puts it another way: "But if we judged ourselves truly, we should not be judged."

These verses suggest that unworthy reception of the sacrament involves thoughtlessness, carelessness, and resistance to the true meaning of the Eucharist. A schismatic spirit or a demeaning of one's fellow believer is inconsistent with the Eucharist. In the same way, not "discerning the Lord's body" may mean both ignoring the mystical body of the Church and failing to assent to the true meaning of Christ's bodily presence. Paul's solution is self-evaluation—"judged ourselves"—so that we won't be condemned with the world (1 Cor. 11:32).

These negatives imply their opposites, too. On the positive side, the believer should be thoughtful, loving, and committed. He must be thoughtful in examining his own relationship with the Church and dedicated to the unity of Christ's mystical body. He must love as Christ calls him to love. And he must be committed to our Lord and his Church. This all suggests that the believer's testing of self and his discerning of the Lord's body carry a strong desire to be united with Jesus and with the Church he established.

So then, how do we approach the Eucharist, practically speaking? The Church helps us by providing many prayers in preparation for Communion. Western Catholics may know the *Anima Christi* and prayers attributed to St. Ambrose and St. Bonaventure as well as to St. Thomas Aquinas. We also find much wisdom in the Eastern side of the Church. In the Byzantine Liturgy of St. John Chrysostom, the "Prayer for Receiving Communion" (the one used most of the liturgical year in the Eastern rites of the Church) has a rich theology of Communion packed into a small compass. Perhaps the most striking feature of this prayer is sincerity. At the end, echoing the thief on the cross who could only beg for mercy, our sincerity in pleading for mercy is what will best prepare us for a worthy reception of Christ.

When we ask God for mercy, we recognize our own sinful tendencies. Thus, in this Byzantine prayer we confess that we are not worthy to enter into the intimacy of a mystical marriage with Christ. And, when we ask that our souls be cleansed, the meaning is essentially the same as a Mass prayer more familiar to Latin-rite Catholics: "Lord, I am not worthy to receive you, but only say the word and I shall be healed."

Prayer for Receiving Communion

(in the Byzantine Liturgy of St. John Chrysostom)
"Lord, I believe and confess that you are truly the Christ, the Son of the Living God.

You came into the world to save sinners of whom I am the first.

I still believe that this is your undefiled body and your precious blood.

So I ask you:

Be merciful to me and forgive my transgressions, both voluntary and involuntary,

Those in word, in action, in knowledge, and in ignorance.

Make me worthy to partake of your pure mysteries without condemnation

For the forgiveness of my sins and for eternal life.

How can I, so unworthy, enter into the splendor of your saints?

If I dare to enter the bridal chamber, my clothes will rebuke me

Since they are not a wedding garment.

I will be seized and tossed out by the angels.

O Lord, lover of the human race, cleanse the filth of my soul and save me.

Loving Master, Lord Jesus Christ, my God,

Let not these holy mysteries be judgment for me because of my unworthiness,

But let them be for the cleansing and holiness of soul and body.

Let them be a pledge of the life to come and of the kingdom.

It is good for me to be united to God and to place my hope of salvation in the Lord.

Today, accept me, O Son of God, as a partaker of your mystical supper.

For I will certainly not tell your mystery to your enemies.

I will not give you a kiss like Judas.

But like the thief I confess, 'Remember me, Lord, in your kingdom.'"

In this personal, moving, and theologically rich prayer, our awareness of our unworthiness becomes more acute as we focus on the purity of Jesus Christ, the Son of God, whose undefiled body we are about to receive. And so Communion includes recognizing the immaculate heart of Jesus as that which is able to cleanse us from our sins. That is why we need him so much, and the prayer allows us to beg Christ that our reception of his body and blood will bring not condemnation but forgiveness.

By receiving the Eucharist, we are given all that is necessary to live a holy life if we avail ourselves of its power. And to better do that, we need to have our hearts well prepared. That is why the Church has a eucharistic fast. Today, that small discipline consists of refraining from food and drink (except water and medicines) for one hour prior to receiving holy Communion. Historically, the period and conditions of the fast have varied, but the purpose has always been the same: to prepare the hearts of the faithful by an act of self-denial that opens up the soul to assimilate such a great gift.

Perhaps you remember when you were young that your mother would not allow you to eat candy or cookies before dinner because she knew that would spoil your appetite for a nutritious meal. Your mother loved you enough to make you deny your impulses for a greater good. At the same time, she was teaching you healthy habits of self-discipline. Our mother the Church cares for us, her children, much the same, asking us to deny ourselves in this small way so that we can be better prepared to receive the life-transforming food of the Eucharist.

How often should one receive Communion? If possible as often as we go to Mass. "It is in keeping with the very meaning of the Eucharist that the faithful, if they have the required dispositions, receive Communion when they participate in the Mass."[20] Since we normally expect to receive Christ in Holy Communion, we should normally prepare by keeping the eucharistic fast and praying for the right inner dispositions so that we may be open to his grace.

DO I NEED TO GO TO RECONCILIATION FIRST?

There are times when it would be improper for an individual to receive Holy Communion. The Eucharist was instituted "for the forgiveness of sins" (Matt. 26:28), and so the Church has consistently taught that this sacrament takes away venial sin. But the Church also teaches us that we cannot be in a state of mortal (that is, grave or serious) sin and receive Communion.

The *Catechism* says, "Anyone conscious of a grave sin must receive the sacrament of reconciliation before coming to Communion."[21] The *Code of Canon Law* notes:

> A person who is conscious of grave sin is not to celebrate Mass (applying to a priest) or to receive the body of the Lord (applying to all) without prior sacramental confession unless a grave reason is present and there is no opportunity of confessing; in this case the person is to be mindful of the obligation to make an act of perfect contrition, including the intention of confessing as soon as possible.[22]

Many people seem confused on the difference between venial and mortal sins and the relation of the two kinds to Communion. There may be many reasons for this uncertainty, including poor

---

Worthy Reception of the Eucharist

"But we must always take care that this great meeting with Christ in the Eucharist does not become a mere habit, and that we do not receive him unworthily, that is to say, in a state of mortal sin. The practice of the virtue of penance and the sacrament of penance [reconciliation] are essential for sustaining in us and continually deepening that spirit of veneration that man owes to God himself and to his love so marvelously revealed."[10]

---

instruction, neglect of the sacrament of reconciliation, or lack of regular self-examination. However, the Church has good reason for commanding that we not receive Communion if we are in a state of mortal sin: It does so for our spiritual health.

The question may arise: If receiving the Eucharist forgives sin, why *shouldn't* we receive Christ for forgiveness even if we are in a state of mortal sin? Because mortal sin cuts us off from Christ and his Church. "Mortal sin destroys charity in the heart of man by a grave violation of God's law; it turns man away from God, who is his ultimate end and beatitude [happiness], by preferring an inferior good to him."[23] Jesus Christ still loves us with an unwavering love, but by choosing to sin mortally, we have turned away from that love in a definitive manner. The flow of Christ's mercy to our souls has been interrupted, and the forgiveness conveyed in the sacrament of reconciliation is necessary to restore it.

Because forgiveness is in Christ himself, why can't we have that through the Eucharist? Receiving the Eucharist means that we are in communion with the Church that Christ founded. If we are in a state of mortal sin, that's not the case. To receive the Eucharist in such a state would be a lie.

What is committing a mortal sin, or being in a state of mortal sin? The Church does not publish a list. That type of reference would be longer than anyone could possibly remember. It would also miss the point that a mortal sin is a matter of the heart as much as it is outward acts of that sin. For a sin to be mortal, three conditions must be met: "Mortal sin is sin whose object is grave matter and is also committed with full knowledge and deliberate consent."[24]

Grave matter is an act against the love of God or love of neighbor. The Ten Commandments are a summary of these two categories. The first three focus on our love of God and last seven have to do with our love of neighbor.[25]

Here's an example.

Suppose a man has a habit of swearing. Maybe he works in a place where he hears coarse language all the time. Maybe he knows that it's not good, but he has a bad habit of it slipping from time to time. Instances of cursing in this environment would not be mortal sin, because he does not fully consent to it when he blurts out something without thinking. However, suppose that same man is angry toward one of his fellow workers and curses him. Before he berates his colleague, he pauses to consider his action but decides to do it anyway. This could be a mortal sin. Why? Tearing into someone that way is a serious act against love of neighbor (grave matter), the swearer was aware that he should not do it (full knowledge), and he freely made a decision to do it anyway (deliberate consent).

Other examples could be given, but it would be more useful to have a few guidelines to keep in mind. Only the person committing the act can know whether the sin is mortal. No one can judge the heart of another person. The Church makes no presumption to do so. The Church can say that "such and such an action" is grave matter. That is the objective side of the question. But only God can judge a person's heart with regard to full knowledge and full consent. Anyone who commits an act, word, or thought that is grave matter can use this guideline to seek forgiveness in the sacrament of reconciliation (confession), and should do so. Yet we must always remember that both sacraments (confession and Eucharist) were given for the same purpose: to receive Christ and his forgiveness so that we may live a holy life.

AFTER COMMUNION: YOUR PERSONAL THANKSGIVING (EUCHARISTIA)

Let's assume that you have prepared yourself well for receiving Christ in Holy Communion. You are not in a state of mortal sin or, if you suspect you are, you have gone to confession to be reconciled to Christ and his Church. You have observed the one-hour fast and have prayed for an open heart. Now you step forward and receive Communion. You have been given the King of kings and the Lord of lords in the most holy sacrament of his body and blood. Is there anything more to do?

Most certainly. And it all begins with your prayer after Communion.

Perhaps an analogy will help. If you are sick and take the medication your physician prescribes, you know that it takes time for it to have its effect. It has to travel through your body to the parts damaged by the illness and begin its healing work. Much the same is true of the Eucharist spiritually, which is one reason Ignatius of Antioch referred to it as "the medicine of immortality."

How can you allow this spiritual remedy to have its effect? The time of prayer after receiving Holy Communion should be a period of letting the reality of Christ's loving presence sink deeply into your soul so that he, the great physician, can heal it of its troubles. Throughout the history of the Church, great saints have emphasized this point. Cyril of Jerusalem understood this when he spoke to his people in fourth-century Jerusalem:

> Then after you have communed in the body of Christ, come also to the cup of his blood, not extending your hands, but kneeling in a posture of worship and reverence. With the "Amen" be sanctified by receiving from Christ's blood. And while your lips are still wet with moisture, sanctify your eyes, your forehead, and your other senses by touching them. Then, waiting in prayer, give thanks to God who made you worthy of such great mysteries.[26]

While Cyril's suggested gestures may not be necessary, he gets to the heart of the importance of internalizing the benefits of receiving the body and blood of Christ. Another great Eastern Father, John Chrysostom, advises:

> You are about to receive the king under your roof in Communion. As the king enters your soul, you should be in much tranquility, much silence, deep peace of thoughts.[27]

The time after Communion should be devoted to quiet prayer and reflection. Bask in the light of Christ's love.

There are many more implications to receiving Holy Communion. For now it is vitally important to use the wisdom of the Church to make the most of our reception of the Blessed Sacrament. Thoughtful preparation and confession of sin, prayerful reflection and meditation, reverent posture, and settled inner disposition will enhance participation in the Eucharist as the healing love of Christ permeates your being. We come as those who wish to love God more by receiving his love in Christ Jesus our Lord. It is no wonder this is a supper for lovers.

6

THE EFFECTS OF
THE EUCHARIST:
TRANSFORMED LIVES

HOLY COMMUNION CREATES the greatest intimacy between Jesus and the believing participant, but the goal of this sacrament goes beyond the act itself. After receiving our Lord, we are only beginning to live the eucharistic life. The time of meditation and thanksgiving allows our hearts to settle upon the beauty of Christ's presence within. However, if that time alone were considered, its larger purpose would be missed. Communion contains within itself the goal of being transformed into the image of Jesus who gives himself to communicants under the appearances of bread and wine.

THE SECOND TRANSFORMATION

During Mass, the act of the priest standing in the place of Christ to change bread and wine into the body and blood of Jesus Christ may be called the *first* transformation, because its purpose is always to lead to a *second* transformation in the lives of those who receive Holy Communion. How does that second change take place?

The process of salvation is an ongoing transformation. In Sacred Scripture, it is called sanctification or justification. Sanctification means setting something apart for a holy purpose; justification is making something right. Both words describe the same reality of the Christian life. Paul summarizes the definitive beginning of this process in one verse. After listing groups of ungodly behaviors, he adds, "And such were some of you. But you were washed [baptized], you were sanctified, you were justified in the name of the Lord Jesus Christ and in the Spirit of our God" (1 Cor. 6:11). The apostle is describing the definitive beginning of the Christian life in three different ways: washing, sanctification, and justification.

The Eucharist continues to nurture what was received in baptism at the beginning of each Christian life. It continues to instill the desire and power to become holier, to draw closer to God, who is the essence of holiness. This process cannot be true or real unless the Christian is also becoming more virtuous and righteous. By a process of inner transformation, the person in true communion with Christ shows that inner reality by a more justified life. By a life of increasing holiness, a process begins by union with Christ. As quoted earlier from the Council of Florence:

> The effect of this sacrament for those who partake worthily is the union of man with Christ. And because a man is incorporated into Christ through grace and united to his members, it follows that through this sacrament grace grows in those who receive worthily. And every effect that material food and drink yields for bodily life—sustaining, growing, healing, delighting—this sacrament works for spiritual life.

The last sentence is taken almost word-for-word from St. Thomas Aquinas's spiritual masterpiece, the *Summa Theologiae*, written about two centuries earlier. Thomas wrote those words[28] as an explanation for why Christ gave us this sacrament in the form of food and drink. He wanted to show the power of invisible realities by linking them closely to something like their natural effects. Whatever effects normal bodily food has, so the Eucharist has the same effects on the soul. Thomas supports this truth by appealing to St. Ambrose ("that bread is for eternal life, which supports the substance of our soul"[29]) and ultimately to the authority of Jesus himself: "For my flesh is food indeed, and my blood is drink indeed" (John 6:55).

We grow in holiness by having the substance of Christ himself to sustain our spiritual lives. Christ's presence in us through the sacrament sustains our hope when we are discouraged, increases our faith when it is faint, heals our faults when they overwhelm us, and sets our hearts right when they are straying from him. All these effects flow from the presence of Christ's Passion in us because the Eucharist unites us to Christ's suffering and death.

The sacrifice of the Mass, embodying Christ's death on the cross, is essential to this process of sanctification. The author of Hebrews helps us to understand this when he writes, "For by a single offering he [Jesus] has perfected for all time those who are sanctified" (Heb. 10:14). Now we see the practical implications of the eucharistic sacrifice. By the offering of his life as a sacrifice for

---

A Completed Job, Continuing Results

The Greek verb tenses used in Hebrews 10:14 are significant. In the one offering of his life, Christ definitively perfected us. The verb "to perfect" occurs in the perfect tense, which means it should be understood as a completed action with continuing results (much as when we say in English, "I have finished the job"). The offering Jesus made is a completed act. But what his self-offering made complete are "those who are sanctified." It implies that the action indicated is an ongoing process.

The author of Hebrews is telling us that we are being made holy in a process that will last our whole lives. The end-point of that process is perfect holiness, complete sanctity. But the entire process has already been accomplished through the sacrificial offering of Christ's body on the cross. From the standpoint of eternity, we have already been sanctified through the offering of Jesus Christ's body once for all (Heb. 10:10).

The upshot of the verses in Hebrews 10 is that all our holiness resides in the body of Jesus Christ. Since it is that same body (sacred humanity) that we receive in the Eucharist, all our holiness—both present and future—is in the Eucharist.

our sins, Jesus Christ already possesses within himself *all* that is needed for our holiness.

In the Mass, the bread and wine are transformed or transubstantiated into the substance of Christ himself. By this means, the sacrifice of the cross enters our hearts and begins its transforming work of making us more into the image of Christ, or as Paul says, "to be conformed to the image of his Son" (Rom. 8:29). The more we receive Christ, the holier we become, which is the essence of sanctification or justification. In the end, Paul's words ring true: "When Christ who is our life appears, then you also will appear with him in glory" (Col. 3:4). This reality holds profound implications for how we view our journey to heaven.

DEIFICATION AND MY GIFT TO THE FATHER

The Fathers of the Church of the East spoke often of deification (sometimes called divinization) as the goal of the Christian life. It is a concept still used by Eastern theologians today. Since this idea is often misunderstood by Western Christians, it requires explanation. The Greek word for deification is *theosis*, which in secular Greek meant a process of becoming more divine. Greek-speaking Christians in the early centuries of the Church adopted this term and filled it with new meaning. They used it to emphasize the growth of the believer who is increasing in the likeness of Christ because, more and more, Jesus is coming into that person's life. This concept is also found in Scripture:

> His divine power has granted to us all things that pertain to life and godliness, through the knowledge of him who called us to his own glory and excellence, by which he has granted to us his precious and very great promises, that through these you may escape from the corruption that is in the world because of the passion, and become partakers of the divine nature (2 Pet.1:3–4).

Becoming "partakers of the divine nature" results from God's power. The gift of the Son of God provides us with all that is necessary for "life and godliness." The purpose of this divine plan is that we may be united completely to God and so live eternally with him. Eternal life commences in this earthly life by the heavenly life of Christ dwelling in us today.

In the Mass, the Church in the West uses different language to speak of the same process:

> Father of mercy,
> in your great love for us
> you have given us your only Son.
> May he take us up into his own perfect sacrifice,
> that we may offer you fitting worship.
> We ask this through Christ our Lord.[30]
> May he make us an everlasting gift to you
> and enable us to share in the inheritance of your saints.[31]

These beautiful words express the desire of the loving servant's heart, the longing for holiness. Too often we feel that holiness eludes us. We are keenly aware of our moral lapses and our spiritual failures. But the words of the liturgy are placed there to turn our eyes away from ourselves to the abundant mercy of God, which takes all our failures, as well as our successes, and unites them to the perfect sacrifice of our Lord. When we pray, "May he make us

---

"By Bending Heaven to Us"

In *The Life of Christ*, fourteenth-century monk Nicholas Cabasilas noted: "In this way [through baptism, confirmation and Eucharist] we live in God. We remove our life from the visible world to that which is not seen. We do so not by exchanging the place but the very life itself and its mode. . . . He did not remove us from here, but he made us heavenly while yet remaining on earth and imparted to us the heavenly life without leading us up to heaven but by bending heaven to us and bringing it down."

---

an everlasting gift to you," we are saying much more than might strike us at first. The Latin sentence behind this English translation is more vivid: *Ipse nos tibi perficiat munus aeternum* (May he himself [Christ] perfect us into an eternal gift to you [the Father]).

This prayer expresses the desire of the Church that the eucharistic Christ would transform those who receive him into a gift, much the same as Jesus himself is a gift to his Father. This is the reverse fulfillment of the people bringing the gifts of bread and wine. They have brought their offerings, made from their hands ("the work of human hands"). Christ the Son has transformed those offerings into the gift of his body and blood as he has acted through the hands and voice of the priest. In Communion, Christ's gift of his body and blood will transform the people of God into a gift that he can present to the Father in heaven.

Further, the wording of this prayer points to a specific kind of change, one that has the goal of perfection. In this regard, the English verb *to make* is an anemic choice for *perficio*, a verb meaning to perfect, complete, or finish. And the choice of *perficio* is not casual or arbitrary, for the substantial transformation of the bread and wine leads to a second transformation of a sinful people into a perfected gift given back to the Father. In both cases, nature is divinized—elevated by divine presence—specifically by the corporeal presence of Christ. The Eternal Word is both gift and giver. He who is given to the people of God himself gives the people back to the Giver.

Thomas Aquinas's prayer after Communion (see appendix 2) wonderfully expresses how the Christian grows in grace through the indwelling presence of Christ in the Eucharist. But how can resistance to evil increase within our souls? The key lies in the increase of virtues. By the expansion of these positive virtues, the negative vices that cling to us will be gradually removed.

> For this very reason make every effort to supplement your faith with virtue, and virtue with knowledge, and knowledge with self-control, and self-control with steadfastness, and steadfastness with godliness, and godliness with brotherly affection, and brotherly affection with love (2 Pet. 1:5–7).

Growing in all the virtues comes out of communicant's partaking in the Eucharist. A person is united with the divine nature through the humanity of Christ. He is empowered to overcome evil and to increase in all the virtues. Because Holy Communion produces peace in an open heart, the communicant is enabled to fight the good fight of faith (1 Tim. 6:12; 2 Tim. 4:7).

DELIVER US FROM THE EVIL ONE

At every Mass, the congregation joins together to say the Our Father (sometimes called the Lord's Prayer), a prayer that may be the most important one in Christian experience, since it comes directly from Christ himself (Matt. 6:5–13). It has always been viewed as the model for all other prayer and has been the subject of a long stream of commentary from the earliest days of the Church. The last petition in this prayer reminds us of the reality of evil in the world: "Deliver us from evil." (In Greek the petition literally reads, "Deliver us from *the* evil," which can mean either "Deliver us from evil" or "Deliver us from the evil one." The Latin is also ambiguous on this point, though the *Catechism of the Catholic Church* links this petition to deliverance from the evil one.)

It is appropriate for the Church gathered at Mass to offer this prayer in unison, since it points us in a fundamental way back to the hope and solution for overcoming evil in our lives. The one who is "our Father" holds the power and will to do away with evil. But if that is true, why do we still have to contend with it? Why do we have to struggle with it in our own lives?

Part of the answer lies in what we have learned about sanctification. Becoming holier requires action from our human will to eradicate the vestiges of sin within us. Since the goal of our lives is to live in an eternal love relationship with God, such a plan can be realized only when our wills freely cooperate with God's grace. If God compelled us against our will, he would not have a love relationship with us. Love supposes the freedom to choose not to love. So, while our sins and imperfections may appear to indicate something lacking in God's method of operation, they really offer further proof of how deeply God desires our returning love to him. He wants us to love him *freely*.

That is why we struggle with evil and sin in our lives. We are not yet perfected in love. We must undergo a process of purification that will last our entire life. If that process is not yet complete at the moment of our death, it will be finished in a final purification known as purgatory.[32]

The realization that we will always struggle with sin in this life leads to two truths:

1. It provides a realistic assessment of ourselves so that we don't imagine that we are better than we are.
2. It causes us to fall back on God's grace every day so that we increasingly live our lives in a way pleasing to him. Relying on God's grace is humility, and humility remains a key to spiritual growth.

What does this have to do with the Eucharist? One of the effects of Communion is the power it gives us to overcome evil in our lives. In traditional theological language, the Eucharist is sometimes called *a remedy against sin*. The Church has long seen the Eucharist as having the power to protect the Christian from sin and temptation. John Chrysostom likened the power of Christ's blood in the Eucharist to the blood of the lambs that was painted on the doors of the children of Israel just before the Passover.

Moses said, "Sacrifice a lamb without blemish and smear the doors with its blood." What does this mean? Can the blood of a sheep without reason save man who is endowed with reason? Yes, Moses replies, not because it is blood but because it is a figure of the Lord's blood. So today if the devil sees not the blood of the figure smeared on the door posts but the blood of the reality smeared on the lips of the faithful, which are the doors of the temple of Christ, with all the more reason will he draw back.[33]

Yet, surely the Eucharist cannot be considered a remedy against sin. Don't we continue to struggle with sin after receiving Holy Communion? We need to remember that overcoming sin in our lives is a lifelong process with many twists, turns, and restarts. There are so many factors involved in this struggle that it would be naive to imagine that there is a simplistic solution. Still, the Eucharist remains our greatest ally and aid in our working toward holiness.

One of the great teachers on this point was St. Bonaventure, a Franciscan, cardinal, and Doctor of the Church. Along with Thomas Aquinas, Bonaventure was one of the greatest theologians of the thirteenth century. In his shortest treatment of Catholic doctrine, called the *Breviloquim*, he titled the section on the sacraments "On the Sacramental Remedy"—an indication of his emphasis on the practical power of the Eucharist.

Bonaventure constantly calls Christ "Our Restoring Principle," indicating that he views the purpose of the sacraments as repairing the damage that original sin has done to us. For him, the sacraments are "disease-healing remedies" that cure the wounds of sin and division. He shows a great awareness that the sacraments are especially fitted for "the fullness of time," because Christ is "full of grace and truth" (John 1:14). This fullness resides in this age of grace because it is the Messianic era, the last great era of redemptive history from an Old Testament perspective. Bonaventure's arguments for the Real Presence rest on this temporal awareness. The nature of the Messianic age demands that the reality of God be on earth and not simply the shadows and signs of the Old Testament times. Still, the theologian insists that this is a time of wayfaring. Even though it is the age of grace and fullness, the times are marked by pilgrimage, not consummation. So the Eucharist continues to function as "sustainment on the way" that fits well with "our state of wayfaring."

How does the Eucharist help the pilgrim in his struggle? How can this sacrament of nourishment really be a force against sin? By changing our desires. As long as we hunger for sin and its deceptive delights, we will not be able to overcome it fully and walk completely in love with God. Bonaventure tells us that the

Eucharist creates an "inner delight through partaking of the pilgrim's food." In effect, as the body and blood of Christ come into us, they alter our orientation by changing our desires. Put simply, we desire to sin less. We must admit openly that such a change of desires does not take place immediately or entirely. It takes time. But then again, that is how love works. It grows through time and exposure. By changing our love, the Eucharist changes our desires.

How does the Eucharist create this "inner delight" within us? Bonaventure says that it inflames our heart with a love for Christ in the same way that Christ's heart burns with love for us. When we burn with desire for someone or something, the object of our love becomes the delight of our soul. Since Christ's person, both body and soul, is fully in the Eucharist, his presence makes our souls long for him in a way that is not naturally possible. The best way for love to grow is by being united with him. Bonaventure summarizes this beautifully:

> This sacrament contains the true body and immaculate flesh of Christ in such a way that it penetrates our being, unites us to one another, and transforms us into him through that burning love by which he gave himself to us, offered himself up for us, and now gives himself back to us, to remain with us until the end of the world.[34]

So, according to Bonaventure, we are gradually enabled to overcome sin in our lives by being in direct union with Christ in the Eucharist. This union creates a bond that burns with love and changes our desires from evil to good. By growing in love with Christ, we grow in delight to please him. The desire to please our Lord engenders within us an aversion to anything that does not please him.

King David of Israel spoke about God's goodness in his famous twenty-third psalm when he wrote: "Thou preparest a table before me in the presence of my enemies" (Ps. 23:5). David could never know the full meaning of his words, but we do. Christ delights our souls with a sumptuous banquet right in front of our worst enemy, the devil. This meal gives us the necessary strength to do battle with the forces of evil that remain within us and allows us to conquer those without. Through Christ who loves us, we become "more than conquerors" (Rom. 8:37).

7

THE EFFECTS OF
THE EUCHARIST:
A SENSE OF MISSION

A PRIEST ONCE spoke about a life-changing experience that forever set the course of his ministry. While he was on a thirty-day Ignatian retreat, he was meditating on the story of Jesus feeding the five thousand (Mark 6:34–44) and began to realize that he wanted his heart to feel compassion in the same way Jesus' heart did. Over time, he began to see the people of the world—the lost sheep—through the merciful eyes of Christ.

That is our goal, too. As we receive Jesus' body and blood, we are to have his sense of purpose in helping others find their way back to the Father. While achieving a greater freedom from sin contains enormous value, to be content with eliminating the negative would only truncate the full intention of Christ in giving us his supper of love. Jesus wants us to have his heart for the world, his love for those "sheep."

DEVELOPING AN APOSTOLIC HEART

One way we know that the Eucharist is having its desired effect in us is by the state of our hearts. When we begin to have a more profound sense of mission, of entering into the redemptive work of Jesus Christ, then we can be sure that the presence of Christ is transforming us. John Paul II emphasized the mission of Christ repeatedly in his writings. His 1990 encyclical *Redemptoris Missio* (Mission of the Redeemer) stressed that everyone in the Church is called to that mission.

The word *mission* derives directly from the Latin *missio*, which means a sending, or a commission. It refers first and foremost to Jesus being sent from the Father in heaven. Consider these eight scriptural passages:

1. For God so loved the world that he gave his only Son, that whoever believes in him should not perish but have eternal life. For God sent the Son into the world, not to condemn the world, but that the world might be saved through him (John 3:16–17).
2. For the works which the Father has granted me to accomplish, these very works which I am doing, bear me witness that the Father has sent me. And the Father who sent me has himself borne witness to me (John 5:36–37).
3. Then they said to him, "What must we do, to be doing the works of God?" Jesus answered them, "This is the work of God, that you believe in him whom he has sent" (John 6:28–29).
4. As the living Father sent me, and I live because of the Father, so he who eats me will live because of me (John 6:57).
5. And this is eternal life, that they know thee the only true God, and Jesus Christ whom thou hast sent (John 17:3).
6. For I have given them the words which thou gavest me, and they have received them and know in truth that I came from thee: and they have believed that thou didst send me (John 17:8).
7. As thou didst send me into the world, so I have sent them into the world (John 17:18).
8. That they may all be one; even as thou, Father, art in me, and I in thee, that they also may be in us, so that the world may believe that thou hast sent me. The glory which thou hast given me I have given to them, that they may be one even as we are one, I in them and thou in me, that they may become perfectly one, so that the world may know that thou hast sent me and has loved them even as thou hast loved me (John 17:21–23).

As you can see, all these passages contain a reference to Jesus as the one sent on a mission. He not only fulfills the Father's plan for the salvation of the world; he is the plan, since eternal life consists of knowing him whom the Father sent. The connection between Jesus being sent by the Father and our own sense of mission comes out particularly in John 17. By knowing the words that Jesus taught, we come to see him as the mission of the Father. Our knowing Christ as the one sent by the Father also leads to our being sent by Christ into the world. The intimate union of these two missions—the Father's in Christ and Christ's in us—climaxes in verses 21–23.

The reason for the Father sending the Son was to bring all God's children into a complete and perfect unity so that those outside the Church may see Jesus as the unifier of humanity ("that the world may know that thou hast sent me"). The unity that Jesus came to give is extraordinary. It is no human invention. This is the uniting of Christ's disciples in the very oneness that binds the Son to the Father ("that they also may be one in us").

Jesus' mission must be our mission, too. Our goal is not just any figment of our imagination; it cannot be just any arbitrary purpose. We are called to the work—the mission—that flows from the depths of the Father's heart, from the same motive that God had in sending his Son into the world. Our mission, like Christ's, consists of bringing the world back into the unity of love that binds the Father, the Son, and the Holy Spirit. That goal is why Jesus gave us himself in the Eucharist.

The fourth passage quoted just above is from John 6, the eucharistic discourse discussed earlier. John 6:57 says, in effect, that Jesus could accomplish his mission only by receiving the Father's life ("I live because of the Father"). So too, Jesus says that we can accomplish our mission only by receiving his life within us ("he who eats me will live because of me"). This truth of feeding on Christ animates and enlivens our mission of bringing our fellow human beings back to God.

You Are What You Receive

Sharing in the mission of Christ also implies that the faithful Catholic is growing in love for the Church as well. Why? Because love for Christ cannot be separated from love for the Church as the body of Christ. We can grasp this better when we understand how the word *body* is used in two closely related senses in Sacred Scripture. On the one hand, in the words of consecration that Jesus first spoke in the institution of the Eucharist ("This is my body"), he refers to his own human body, or more broadly, his whole humanity. On the other hand, Paul uses the "body of Christ" as a figure of speech to talk about the Church.

The apostle includes the word *body* (*soma*) more than eighty times in his letters, using it in several different senses. He refers to the Church as the body of Christ in Romans 12:4–7, in the lengthy 1 Corinthians 12, and in several chapters throughout Ephesians and Colossians. In Romans 12 and 1 Corinthians 12, Paul stresses that each member of the Church has an important role to play in fostering the growth of the Church. By putting the graces we receive to work, we can build up the whole body of Christ. In Romans 12:6 Paul writes, "Having gifts that differ according to the grace given to us, let us use them." The word translated as "gifts" is *charismata* or graces. God's grace is manifold and varied (Eph. 3:10). Each member of the Church can teach or serve or encourage

---

Making It Possible to Persevere

"Were it not for the constant presence of our divine Master in our humble chapel, I would not have found it possible to persevere in sharing the lot of the lepers in Molokai," remarked Blessed Damian de Veuster of Molokai (in the Hawaiian Islands). "The Eucharist is the bread that gives strength. . . . It is at once the most eloquent proof of his love and the most powerful means of fostering his love in us. He gives himself every day so that our hearts as burning coals may set afire the hearts of the faithful."

---

or share, and so on. All these functions come from one source: the grace of God in Jesus.

While Paul's use of *body* in 1 Corinthians recognizes the diverse forms of grace within the Church, he also emphasizes that all come from "the same Spirit . . . the same Lord . . . the same God" (1 Cor. 12:4–6). He stresses unity because of the divisions that threatened the Church in Corinth. But all the gifts, graces, and services performed by the different members of the Church are for one purpose: to bind the Church together. In the same way that the human body has many parts and yet works in a coordinated manner, so, too, must the Church.

The metaphor of the body of Christ for the Church is more than a literary device. In Paul's theology, the Church as the body of Christ is more than analogy. The Church is not only like a human body (though it is that, too); it is a visible embodiment of Christ's personal body as well. One is an extension of the other. The humanity of Jesus is *in* the members of the Church and expressed *through* its members.

That reality of Christ's dwelling in the Church is why Paul heard Jesus say on the day of his conversion on the Damascus road, "Saul, Saul, why do you persecute me?" When Paul asked who was speaking, the voice replied, "I am Jesus, whom you are persecuting" (Acts 9:4–5). Paul was attacking the Church, the followers of Jesus, but he hears the word *me* because to persecute the Church is to persecute Jesus. If Paul understood the phrase "body of Christ" as only an analogy, he might have easily thought that the Church was not Jesus but only a body of people who were like Jesus. But the actual language used suggests that there is an identification between Jesus and the Church as his body.

Many early theologians understood this identification. Among them was Fulgentius of Ruspe, a disciple of St. Augustine:

> So if you wish to understand the body of Christ, hear the apostle speaking to believers, "You are the body of Christ and his members" (1 Cor. 12:27). So if you are the body of Christ and its members, the mystery of who you are is on the Lord's table; you receive the mystery of the Lord. You respond with "Amen"

to what you are and by responding you assent. You hear, "The body of Christ" and you respond, "Amen." Be a member of Christ's body that the "Amen" may be true.[35]

Fulgentius does a good job reflecting Paul's theology of the Church. We are the body of Christ because we receive his body from the table he set for us (1 Cor. 10:17). Our obligation is to make true our "Amen" at Communion time by living out the reality of Christ's body, the Church. Loving the Christ of the Eucharist leads naturally to loving the Church, because the body of Christ dwells in the Church and makes the Church his body. The faithful, as members of the body of Christ, are called to develop the heart of Christ for the needs of the Church.

In 1 Corinthians 14–16 Paul emphasizes that every member of the Church is essential, but in this passage he especially shows how no member of the Church is of less value than another. The key point of this section says:

> But God has so composed the body, giving the greater honor to the inferior part, that there may be no discord in the body, but that the members may have the same care for one another. If one member suffers, all suffer together; if one member is honored, all rejoice together (1 Cor. 12:24–26).

Paul's words are most exemplified in the life of Jesus. Our Lord suffered for the members of his body, and we are called to do the same. We are asked to use our gifts and talents to build up the body of Christ. Scripture includes another prime model for us. By seeing ourselves as agents of the graces flowing to the world, we can follow Mary's example of bearing the Son of God to others (Luke 1:39–45). We can begin to realize that as a member of Christ's body, the Church, we can become the conduit of the many graces that the Church and the world need.

In one of the most important twentieth-century encyclicals on the Church, Pius XII showed the indispensable role that the Church plays in the distribution of God's graces:

As he hung upon the cross, Christ Jesus not only appeased the justice of the eternal Father, which had been violated, but he also won for us, his brethren, an ineffable flow of graces. It was possible for him of himself to impart these graces to mankind directly, but he willed to do so only through a visible Church made up of men, so that through it all might cooperate with him in dispensing the graces of redemption. As the Word of God willed to make use of our nature, when in excruciating agony he would redeem mankind, so in the same way throughout the centuries he makes use of the Church that the work begun might endure.[36]

Pius XII understood and fostered the teaching of Paul. He saw clearly the indispensable role that the Church plays as a co-redeemer with Christ. (Co-redemption means working with Christ in his plan of salvation.) The Church assists bringing the graces from heaven into this sin-filled world so that others may experience that grace as well. Christ chose the Church, his mystical body nourished by his real body, to be the agent of reconciliation among humanity. The Church—with all its warts, blemishes, and faults—is still God's chosen instrument of grace for the world. And as each member receives one grace after another (John 1:16), he becomes an essential instrument in distributing those graces to the other members of the Church and to the world.

IS EUCHARISTIC ADORATION FOR YOU?

There was a priest who prayed that he would come to have a heart like Jesus' heart. We have seen that this privilege, which is beyond words, means to have a sense of Christ's mission. It's a grace that elevates our human efforts into the realm of the divine. In our own time, many people seem to desire this gift, but many more apparently know very little about attaining it. How can you begin to have a heart like Jesus' heart? How can you have a heart *more* like Jesus' heart?

At first glance, the answer the Church gives may seem like the exact opposite of what you need. In some ways, developing that sense of Jesus' mission requires less than we might imagine. In others, it demands more than we may be ready to receive. It calls for a constant union with Christ.

Here we turn to Peter Julian Eymard, that great "apostle of the Eucharist." He wisely counseled two means of fostering our union with Christ: sacramental communion and a life of recollection. It's clear what the first means, but what about the second? Recollection is the art of living in the presence of God constantly, of doing what Paul advised, to "pray constantly" (1 Thess. 5:17). But in our hectic world of stress and immediate gratification, how can one hope to live like that? How can one even *begin* to live like that?

To do the will of God in this world, we each must extend the transforming power of the Eucharist into a life of recollection. One of the most effective methods of doing that is adoring Christ in the Blessed Sacrament. In his 1965 encyclical on the Blessed Sacrament entitled *Mysterium Fidei* (Mystery of Faith), Pope Paul VI spoke about the effects of that kind of prayer:

No one can fail to understand that the divine Eucharist bestows upon the Christian people an incomparable dignity. Not only while the sacrifice is offered and the sacrament is received, but as long as the Eucharist is kept in our churches and oratories, Christ is truly the Emmanuel, that is, "God with us." Day and night he is in our midst, he dwells with us, full of grace and

---

Proclaiming What We Revere

"If the sacrament of the Lord's passion is to work its effect in us, we must imitate what we receive and proclaim to mankind what we revere. The cry of the Lord finds a hiding place in us if our lips fail to speak of this, though our hearts believe in it. So that his cry may not lie concealed in us, it remains for us all, each in his own measure, to make known to those around us the mystery of our new life in Christ."[11]

---

truth (John 1:14). He restores morality, nourishes virtues, consoles the afflicted, strengthens the weak. He proposes his own example to those who come to him that all may learn to be, like himself, meek and humble of heart and to seek not their own interests but those of God.[37]

The Holy Father referred to a proven method of fulfilling Christ's mission. As each member of the Church adores the eucharistic Christ more and more, he is empowered to become the salt and light for the world that Jesus said he should be (Matt. 5:13–16). On the surface, such contemplative prayer may not seem like an effective strategy for doing God's work, but in fact it is the fuel that powers the engine of our witness.

8

THE EFFECTS OF THE EUCHARIST: UNION WITH THE WHOLE CHURCH

THE JESUS WE receive in the Eucharist is forever the God-Man in one person. Because he is unique as the Son of God and the Son of Man, it is tempting to think that maybe these two natures, divinity and humanity, can be separated. In fact, that is exactly what some heretics in the early Church thought. But the Church wisely saw that if Jesus' divinity and humanity were separated, he could no longer be the Savior of the human race. Salvation is union with God, and this could take place only through one who unites humanity and divinity in his own person. Jesus Christ cannot be divided or separated from himself.

What is true of Christ is true of Christ's Church as well. As the Church is Christ's body, then it cannot be divided any more than he can be divided. This may not seem to be the case at all since there are many different Christian denominations in the world. After all, isn't the body of Christ divided into churches that number in the thousands? The appearance of many different churches all claiming to be true to Christ is exactly that: an appearance. The reality is that Christ intended only one Church, which he will not allow to be divided any more than his physical body can be divided. The link is between the unity of the Eucharist and the unity of the Church of Christ.

Earlier, we learned that the body of Christ is more than a mere metaphor. The real body of Christ dwells in the members of his mystical body. In the Eucharist, Christ gives us his real body under the appearances of bread and wine. This real body feeds his mystical body and communicates his own unity to it.

THE SACRAMENT OF UNITY

One of the many traditional terms for the Eucharist is "the sacrament of unity." It has been called that because it both signifies and seals the unity of the Church. In our own time, the liturgy constantly reminds us of that in its eucharistic prayers:

> We offer them [the gifts] for your holy Catholic Church.
> Watch over it, Lord, and guide it,
> grant it peace and unity throughout the world.[38]
> May all of us who share in the body and blood of Christ
> be brought together in unity by the Holy Spirit.[39]
> Grant that we, who are nourished by his body and blood,
> may be filled with the Holy Spirit,
> and become one body, one spirit in Christ.[40]
> Lord, look upon this sacrifice which you have given to your
> Church;
> and by your Holy Spirit, gather all who share this one bread
> and one cup
> into the one body of Christ, a living sacrifice of praise.[41]

You can see that each prayer reflects the intimate union between Christ's personal body and his Church. Each reminds us that the purpose of the Eucharist is to unite all God's children into a deeper unity of faith, hope, and love. When we receive Christ in Communion, we have the seeds of unity within us.

The biblical foundations for these prayers can be found in Paul's teaching:

> Therefore, my beloved, shun the worship of idols. I speak as to
> sensible men; judge for yourselves what I say. The cup of blessing
> which we bless, is it not a participation in the blood of Christ?
> The bread which we break, is it not a participation in the body
> of Christ? Because there is one bread, we who are many are one
> body, for we all partake of the one bread (1 Cor. 10:14–17).

The two questions Paul asks are mentioned in the context of deal-
ing with idolatry. He does not want the Christians in Corinth to be
involved in the pagan temples. If they eat the ritual meals at the altars there, they will be associating themselves with false religion. In
contrast is eating at the table of the Lord. Such sharing associates
them with Christ by way of participation in his body and blood.

The final verse in this passage adds another reason for eating
only at the Lord's table. The many members of the Church are
drawn into the one body of Christ by partaking of the one and the
same bread. Examine the language carefully. "Because there is one
bread" seems on the surface to be absurd. Surely, with all the different congregations in Paul's day, there were many different loaves
of bread on many different altars. Yet, Paul says that "there is one
bread." Further, what makes the Church one is that all its members partake of the same loaf? How can all those loaves in all those
churches be "one" and also make the partakers one? This could be
true only because the bread has really become the body of Christ,
the wine has really become his blood. Paul is clearly teaching that
the Eucharist is, in fact, an instrument to draw the members of
the Church more closely into the mystical body of Christ. The
source of unity with the whole Church lies in the body and blood
of Christ.

Why did our Lord choose that specific food and that specific
drink as the visible means through which to convey his true body
and blood? We learn from the wisdom of the Church Fathers. As
noted, the *Didache* is one of the earliest Christian documents outside the New Testament and as such is a very early witness to the
faith of the Church. In one of its eucharistic prayers prescribed for

pastors, the author implied that the Eucharist signaled the unity of the Church:

> Concerning the broken bread, pray like this: We thank you, our Father, for life and knowledge that you have made known to us through Jesus your child. To you be the glory forever. As the broken bread was scattered on the mountains and then gathered into one, thus let your church be gathered from the ends of the earth into your kingdom because yours is the glory and the power through Jesus Christ forever.[42]

> Remember, Lord, your Church, to rescue it from every evil and to make it perfect in your love, and gather it from the four winds, completely sanctified into your kingdom that you have prepared.[43]

With the words "the broken bread was scattered on the mountains and then gathered into one," perhaps the writer is thinking of the multiplication of the fish and loaves as recorded in Mark 6:32–44 (cf. Matt. 14:13–21; 15:32–39; Mark 8:1–10; Luke 9:11–17; John 6:5–13). He sees a parallel between the scattering of the loaves and the dispersing of the Church. The diversity and multiplicity of the Church did not need to be emphasized; that was obvious. But the author also observes a parallel between the collection of the leftover loaves (Mark 6:43) and the gathering of the Church. The Church is to be more and more one as it moves toward the eternal kingdom. This text shows how early in the history of the Church its leaders prayed for unity in the celebration of the Eucharist. And as we can see in the eucharistic prayers used in our own time, Catholic worship still follows that same pattern.

That link between the unity of the Church and the Eucharist grew even stronger over time as the early Fathers continued to reflect on the Lord's choice of bread and wine. St. Cyprian of Carthage, the ancient "apostle of unity," commented on this point in a letter:

But the church cannot be outside itself, not torn or divided against itself. Rather, as the divine faith in Scripture makes clear, it holds the unity of an inseparable and undivided house, since it is written of the sign of the Passover and of the Lamb who represents Christ, "it shall be eaten in one house; you shall not throw the flesh outside the house" (Ex. 12:46). Finally, the sacrifices of the Lord declare a Christian unanimity joined to a firm and inseparable love. For when the Lord calls the bread his body brought together by the joining of many grains, he is indicating our united people whom he carries. And when he calls the wine his blood, squeezed out of many grapes . . . and meshed into one, he signifies our flock joined together by a mixture of a united multitude.[44]

Cyprian wrote these words in a time when various leaders were trying to split the Church by breaking off into their own groups. He might have responded by exhorting them not to cut the body of Christ into bits and pieces, but he makes another point instead. The Church cannot be divided. Individuals may abandon the Church, but that does not mean that the Church has been divided. An analogy is marriage. If a husband abandons his wife, that does not mean that the spouses' marriage is dissolved. He is still married to the woman even if he refuses to acknowledge it. Cyprian is saying much the same of the Church.

As proof of the indivisibility of the Church, Cyprian calls attention to the nature of bread and wine. Both are a combination of natural elements (grains, grapes) and human work. The natural is the divine element, and the work to make these into bread and wine is the human contribution. Cyprian sees the combination of these elements as symbolic of the unity of the Church.

More than two centuries later, we still find theologians making that link between the Eucharist and the unity of the Church. This from Fulgentius:

So why is it in bread? Here we claim nothing of ourselves. Let's hear the apostle himself again. When he speaks about that sacrament, he says, "One bread, we who are many are one body" (1 Cor. 10:17). Understand and rejoice! Unity, devotion, truth, charity, one bread, we who are many are one body. Consider that the bread is not made from one grain but from many. . . . It is like this: To make the appearance of visible bread, many grains are scattered into one like what Holy Scripture says about the faithful: "They had one soul and heart in God" (Acts 4:32).

Understand also, brothers, about the wine and from where it becomes one. Many grains hang together as grapes, but the liquid of the grains are brought together in unity. Thus, the Lord Jesus Christ shows us that he wanted us to relate it to him. He consecrated the mystery of our peace and unity in his table. Whoever receives the mystery of unity and does not preserve the bond of peace does not receive it as a mystery for himself but as a testimony against himself.[45]

In our own time, John Paul II extended this teaching in his encyclical *Ecclesia de Eucharistia*. His opening sentence captures the essence of his thought: "The Church draws her life from the Eucharist." How? The Blessed Sacrament is the preeminent connection between the Church and the paschal mystery. Because the Church is "born of the paschal mystery," every celebration brings us back to the cross and to Jesus' death. As he reflects on 1 Corinthians 10:17, John Paul notes that union with the mystery of Christ's death and resurrection has profound implications for understanding the unifying power of the Eucharist. The unity of the Church is bound up with the paschal mystery, which is reenacted and re-presented in every eucharistic celebration:

Union with Christ, which is a gift and grace for each of us, makes it possible for us, in him, to share in the unity of his body that is the Church. The Eucharist reinforces the incorporation into Christ that took place in baptism through the gift of the Spirit (cf. 1 Cor. 12:13).[46]

How does the Eucharist strengthen our membership and involvement in the Church? It draws our hearts into the mystery of the Church. And the mystery of the Church consists in its being a living sign of Christ in the world. John Paul's teaching extends that of the Second Vatican Council's, that "the Church, in Christ, is in the nature of a sacrament, that is, of communion with God and of unity among all men."[47] The Church knows full well that "it remains for them [humanity] to achieve full unity in Christ" and so its mission is to bring about that unity through its mission of preaching the gospel. That mission, as we have already seen, is fueled by participating in the eucharistic Christ.

John Paul is saying that every member of the Church has a special role in working toward unity, because all share in Christ through Holy Communion. His words reiterate the Second Vatican Council's *Unitatis Redintegratio* (Decree on Ecumenism):

> The longing for restoring unity involves the whole Church, faithful and clergy alike. It extends to everyone, according to the talent of each, whether it be exercised in daily Christian living or in theological and historical studies. The desire itself already reveals to some extent the bond of brotherhood existing among all Christians, and it leads toward full and perfect unity, in accord with what God in his kindness wills.[48]

Both the Council and the Pope connect greater unity within the Church and with other Christians to a continual reform of the life of the Church.[49] No matter how lowly or insignificant we may think our position is, we can each contribute to greater unity because each of us who receive Christ in the Eucharist take in the principle and power of unity within ourselves. When we pray at Mass that we may "be brought together in unity" and "become one body, one spirit in Christ," we are praying that our lives may demonstrate the unity of Christ that has been given to us in the Blessed Sacrament.

Unity with Our Pastors

There's even more to the connection between the Eucharist and unity. Being in union with Christ also means that we are in union with those whom Christ has appointed as his undershepherds for his Church. We are reminded of this at every Mass when we pray:

> Lord, remember your Church throughout the world.
> Make us grow in love
> together with [Name], our Pope,
> [Name], our bishop, and all the clergy.[50]

This prayer indicates that union with the Church requires an attitude of humility and a willingness to be obedient to the validly ordained pastors of Christ's flock. The apostles themselves gave this counsel in the New Testament:

- "Remember your leaders, those who spoke to you the word of God; consider the outcome of their life, and imitate their faith" (Heb. 13:7).
- "Likewise, you that are younger be subject to the elders. Clothe yourselves, all of you, with humility toward one another" (1 Pet. 5:5).

Ignatius on Unity

"Therefore, it is fitting that you agree with the opinion [or will] of the bishop as you are doing. Your rightly famous presbytery [body of priests] is worthy of God. It is in harmony with the bishop like strings tuned to a harp. For this reason, Jesus Christ is praised in your harmony and in your united love."[12]

"Therefore, be diligent to employ only one Eucharist. For there is only one flesh of our Lord Jesus Christ and there is only one cup for unity in his blood. There is one altar as there is one bishop together with the presbytery and the deacons, my fellow servants. The purpose of all this is so that your practices will be in accord with God's intention."[13]

These exhortations are based on the fact that Christ appointed the apostles as the first bishops (*bishop* means overseer) of the Church, and they in turn appointed others to succeed them.

History shows that the faithful have always had problems with obedience to bishops and priests. As Ignatius (one of the earliest bishops of Antioch, in Syria) was being escorted to Rome for trial, he wrote to several faith communities in Asia Minor who were having problems with following their appointed leaders. He urged these Christians to remember their obligations:

Ignatius weaves together several important threads. He entices us to see harmony in the Church as a beautiful reality that brings praise to Jesus Christ. We should eschew all disunity and dissension within God's Church. Schism is a sin against love. But how do we promote harmony? By always trying to act in accord with our bishop. We cannot pray for our pope and bishop while at the same time living in disobedience to them. Such a life is faith without works, which, as St. James says, is dead faith (Jas. 2:17).

But notice, too, how Ignatius connects the Eucharist with this obedience: "That Eucharist should be considered valid that is under the authority of a bishop or under one he has appointed." Holding liturgy in union with our bishops assures us that our Eucharist is valid, that it really becomes the body and blood of Christ. The Eucharist symbolizes the unity of the Church and, therefore, should be celebrated in a way that points to unity and harmony.

In modern times, Catholic teaching has reaffirmed the importance of union with Christ's mystical body through recognizing the visible head of the Church. This point cannot be stressed too much, especially in the United States. Since the sixteenth century, all too many Western Christians have gradually accepted the idea that the Church is primarily an invisible body of believers who need not have a common governmental structure. In this view, Jesus did not found an institution but only a loose body of believers who freely ordered their churches as they saw best.

For people who hold this perspective, the early Church was nothing like the Catholic Church. It had no pope, no bishops, no priests. Most of all, it had no real authority. This view has become pervasive even in many Catholic circles among people who naively trust what some historical scholars say about early Christian history. (I once held this view myself as a Presbyterian theological professor and minister. But my own research into the historical documents of the early Church convinced me otherwise.)

Ignatius is an example of one who teaches a hierarchical Church structure from the very earliest Christian times. But it is against the background of this kind of thinking that modern Catholic teaching has been forced to remind us that the structure of authority in the Church is not a manmade construction. It is a divine ordering given by Jesus Christ. That needed to be emphasized by Pope Leo XIII in the late nineteenth century when this kind of thinking became prominent. In his encyclical *Satis Cognitum*, Leo XIII stressed that the Church is unlike any other human society or organization on earth:

The Church's "Visible Foundation Stone"

"But we must not think that he [Christ] rules only in a hidden or extraordinary manner. On the contrary, our Redeemer also governs his mystical body in a visible and normal way through his vicar on earth. . . . After he had ruled the 'little flock' during his mortal pilgrimage, Christ our Lord, when about to leave this world and return to the Father, entrusted to the chief of the apostles the visible government of the entire community he had founded. Since he was all wise he could not leave the body of the Church he had founded as a human society without a visible head. . . . After his glorious ascension into heaven this Church rested not on him alone but on Peter, too, its visible foundation stone. They, therefore, walk in the path of dangerous error who believe that they can accept Christ as the head of the Church while not adhering loyally to his vicar on earth. They have taken away the visible head, broken the visible bonds of unity, and left the mystical body of the Redeemer so obscured and so maimed that those who are seeking the haven of eternal salvation can neither see it nor find it."[14]

> The Church is visible because it is a body. Hence they err in a matter of divine truth who imagine the Church to be invisible, intangible, a something merely pneumatological as they say, by which many Christian communities, though they differ from each other in their profession of faith, are united by an invisible bond.[51]

Leo is countering the view that many different churches could be unified even though they disagree in doctrine. Without a common profession of faith, there can be no true unity. The Church has an invisible and a visible aspect, but the error of this thinking is that these two could be separated completely.

When Pius XII turned his attention to teaching on the mystical body of Christ, he, too, stressed that the invisible should never be severed from the visible. He put the matter squarely. We have an emaciated conception of the Church if we think that it is only invisible or without governmental structure. Its structure is from Jesus himself and, therefore, disobedience to the Church is disobedience to Christ. The Eucharist is a call to obedience, not only to Christ but also to the Church that Christ founded.

This unity means that the Mass must never be considered a private exercise to be determined by our own lights. No priest is free to make up the Mass in any way he chooses. He has inherited it from the past ages through the authority of his bishop. To change, alter, or denude the Mass of its symbolism and meaning is a serious sin against Christ and a violation of Church law. Much less should the Mass be used for political purposes, whether civic or ecclesiastical. The Eucharist is much too precious and valuable to become the battle ground for petty jealousies.

To receive the Eucharist is a profession of one's faith and agreement with the Church's teaching. Although many in our day don't understand this, it is hypocrisy to receive Communion and then proceed to disobey or publicly disagree with the Church's official teachings. Being a Catholic means believing that all the Church teaches is taught by God through the instrumentality of the Church. It means believing that the Church is God's chosen vessel for instructing us in the faith.

However, that doesn't mean that we might not struggle with certain teachings of the Church. Perhaps we might not understand a teaching or have certain emotional obstacles to trusting the Church. These are delicate pastoral needs that should not be treated carelessly. But our intention should always be to think with the Church in its teaching and action. The holy, Catholic Church was established by Christ, the eternal Son of God. Our communion with him in the holy Eucharist must be matched by a communion with his Church.

9

THE EFFECTS OF THE EUCHARIST: LIVING A SACRAMENTAL LIFE EVERY DAY

ONE OF THE greatest dangers in studying the Eucharist—or any truth in theology—is the temptation to separate it from the fabric of our daily lives. But this great gift was not meant to be limited to a weekly or even a daily ritual. Christ intended it to be "the source and summit of the Christian life."[52]

Our Christianity is lived in the everyday world of jobs, family, education, business, and relationships. But how does a more profound eucharistic life shape our everyday decisions of paying the bills, raising children, juggling obligations, and pursuing careers?

One of the ironies of our busy lives is that we spend so much time on matters that are of so little importance. As we grow in wisdom, age, and grace, we often come to realize that what matters most are the relationships we sustain with other people. Success or failure in business, education, finances come to mean less and less. We come to care more and more about the human beings around us. So, what difference does our knowledge of the Eucharist make in our human relationships? And how can our love for Christ in this sacrament touch the lives of the people around us?

Those questions are also the ones God asks us, the ones God asks *of* us. He wants us to live our lives out of the love and strength he provides in the Eucharist. He wants to teach us the intimate connection between love of God and love of our fellow human beings. In the end, these are what matters most. Perhaps that is why the teaching of Christ in the New Testament focuses on two priorities that we are tempted to neglect: love of the poor and reconciliation with our enemies.

CONCERN FOR THE NEEDY

One way we help lead others back to the love of God is by showing his love to those in need. When Jesus was asked, "Which commandment is the first of all?" (Mark 12:28) and "What good deed must I do, to have eternal life?" (Matt. 19:16), he gave the same two answers:

"Hear, O Israel: The Lord our God, the Lord is one; and you shall love the Lord your God with all your heart, and with all your soul, and with all your mind, and with all your strength" (Mark 12:29–30). No Jew of Jesus' day would have disputed his reply, which quoted Deuteronomy 6:4 5. Long before the time of Christ it had been commonly accepted as Israel's confession of faith and highest obligation (Luke 10:26).

"You shall love your neighbor as yourself" (Mark 12:31). Noting that the second flowed from the first, Jesus was quoting Leviticus 19:18. Again, he was reaffirming what every knowledgeable Jew of his day should have known: In God's plan, love of God is inseparable from love of neighbor.

The truth that sets Jesus' answer apart from all that the Jews had known up to that time is his definition of *neighbor*. It is one that becomes obvious in his now-familiar parable of the good Samaritan (Luke 10:25–37).

The inspired writers of the New Testament confirm that, in the world, love of neighbor is the means for expressing love of God. John warns that love of God and hatred toward human beings are incompatible:

We know that we have passed out of death into life, because we love the brethren. He who does not love abides in death. . . . If anyone has the world's goods and sees his brother in need, yet closes his heart against him, how does God's love abide in him? Little children, let us not love in word or speech but in deed and in truth (1 John 3:14, 17–18).

If any one says, "I love God," and hates his brother, he is a liar; for he who does not love his brother whom he has seen, cannot love God whom he has not seen. And this commandment we have from him, that he who loves God should love his brother also (1 John 4:20–21).

The apostle James also demonstrates that any claims to faith are inseparable from love for those in need:

If a brother or sister is ill-clad and in lack of daily food, and one of you says to them, "Go in peace, be warmed and filled," without giving them the things needed for the body, what does it profit (Jas. 2:15–16)?

These passages point us to the practical implications of the Eucharist. If Christ truly communicates his love to us through the consecrated bread and wine, then our whole life can and should become eucharistic. Such a life works out love of God and love of neighbor in the concrete situations of everyday life. As his body is food for the life of the world (John 6:51), so our lives are broken in service to humanity. We, the members of the Church, are his body, but we also learn to see Christ's broken body in the needs of those around us. John Chrysostom saw the intimate connection between Christ's sacramental body and his embodiment in the poor:

Would you honor the body of Christ? Do not despise his nakedness; do not honor him here in church clothed in silk vestments and then pass him by unclothed and frozen outside. Remember that he who said, "This is my body" and made good his words, also said, "You saw me hungry and gave me no food," and "insofar as you did it not to one of these, you did it not to me."

In the first sense the body of Christ does not need clothing but worship from a pure heart. In the second sense it does need clothing and all the care we can give it.[53]

John Chrysostom takes seriously Jesus' words in the parable of the sheep and the goats in Matthew 25:31–46. So should we. Jesus' description of Judgment Day reminds us that by caring for those broken in body and spirit, we are in fact caring for Christ himself, since he lives in the needy in a special way.

In our own time, we use the phrase "preferential option for the poor" to describe this biblical and patristic morality of love. We need this reminder that social justice is an integral part of evangelization because not a few people in the Church have a tendency to separate social justice and preaching the gospel. But when we sever one from the other—emphasizing social justice to the exclusion of gospel proclamation or stressing proclamation to the exclusion of meeting social needs—we have committed that unacceptable divorce of faith and works, which James condemns (Jas. 2:14–26).

Who and where are the poor in today's world? In what ways are they poor? We know that poverty comes in many forms, both near and far. It is all around us:

• Those who do not have the basic necessities of life
• Those who have their dignity taken from them through ill-treatment
• Those impoverished in mind through lack of education
• Those deprived of a meaningful life because they have been swept up by consumerism (even among the materially rich there is a poverty of the heart)
• Those deprived of life before they even emerge from their mothers' wombs.

There is also great material poverty we may have never seen first-hand because we have been insulated from the everyday realities of poor countries. If you have ever traveled to a third world country and witnessed the deprivation there, you know the huge difference between the material wealth most of us enjoy in North America and the lack of basic services—such as running water and plumbing—in other places.

A few years ago I was speaking at several churches in the Caribbean. On some of the islands there was a stark contrast between the plush resorts where Europeans and Americans vacationed and the small, native towns—less than a mile away—where the people lived in squalor.

That's not to say we have to travel far to see the poor. Let me give a personal example. I teach at a university ranked among the top fifty nationwide. Most of my students are very bright, and many have enjoyed a solid high school education. Many of these young men and women are highly motivated to succeed. A few years ago I began feeling that I should change my lifestyle by leaving my job and beginning some form of service to the poor and disadvantaged. I started praying that God would show me how to move from the world of the privileged few to be among those in need.

As I prayed, I began to notice a poverty among the students. Many of them are pursuing courses of study and careers for no real purpose other than that it is what is expected of them. They seem to have no idea what a vocation from God is. Many are living empty lives without any spiritual purpose. Many do not know

---

The School of Active Love for Neighbor

"The authentic sense of the Eucharist becomes of itself the school of active love for neighbor. We know that this is the true and full order of love that the Lord has taught us: 'By this love you have for one another, everyone will know that you are my disciples.' The Eucharist educates us to this love in a deeper way; it shows us, in fact, what value each person, our brother or sister, has in God's eyes if Christ offers himself equally to each one under the species of bread and wine. If our eucharistic worship is authentic, it must make us grow in awareness of the dignity of each person. The awareness of that dignity becomes the deepest motive of our relationship with our neighbor."[15]

even the basics of the Catholic faith even though they may have attended Mass most of their lives. They are deprived of meaning, poor in knowledge, and at the mercy of nihilistic philosophies. In some respects, they lack more than many who have only a tenth of their material possessions. It became clearer to me that God had placed the "poor" in my classes. I saw them walking across the campus quad. I heard tales of them partying until they dropped. In short, I saw that my university was full of poor people.

Those of us who are privileged to receive the living God, Jesus Christ, in the Blessed Sacrament are called to serve the poor. If we cannot see their poverty, it is only because we have not asked to see it. When we ask to see with Jesus' eyes, we will begin finding the poor everywhere.

RECONCILIATION WITH OUR ENEMIES

As we begin to better understand the true meaning of the Eucharist, it can start to seem somewhat natural for us to be concerned about the poor and needy. But the gospel of Christ's love contained in the Blessed Sacrament goes even further: It calls us to reconciliation with our enemies. There is nothing natural about this more radical step, at least not in a world so affected by sin. We followers of Christ are called to greater love than is humanly possible. In the

The Reflection of His Own Fatherly Care

"Let us now extend to the poor and those afflicted in different ways a more open-handed generosity so that God may be thanked through many voices and the relief of the needy supported by our fasting. No act of devotion on the part of the faithful gives God more pleasure than that which is lavished on his poor. Where he finds charity with its loving concern, there he recognizes the reflection of his own fatherly care."[16]

final analysis, we are called to a love that alone can heal the wounds of sin and division among humanity.

We are reminded of this at every Mass when, right after the Our Father, we share a "Sign of Peace." This has been a part of the breaking of the bread since the very beginning. It can be found in Justin Martyr's description of the Mass dating from the mid-second century.[54] Why has this exchange of peace between the priest and the congregation, and among members of the congregation, remained so important? It is based on our Lord's teaching:

> So if you are offering your gift at the altar, and there remember that your brother has something against you, leave your gift there before the altar and go; first be reconciled to your brother, and then come and offer your gift (Matt. 5:23–24).

Because reconciliation is paramount, Jesus says our worship is worthless if we are at odds with our fellow human beings. The Mass has the exchange of peace as a symbolic gesture that reminds us that we must not harbor hatred or burning anger toward anyone when we come to the Eucharist. If we are at enmity with anyone, the greeting of peace tells us of our need to reconcile with that person as soon as possible.

Although reconciliation with a brother or sister is not a condition of receiving Communion, if we take Christ's words in Matthew 5:23–24 seriously and are in an unreconciled state with a brother or sister—barring circumstances or situations beyond our means—maybe we should not receive the Eucharist. After all, he did say that we should first go and be reconciled *before* offering our gifts. That is a possibility, especially if our hatred is long-standing or is deep-seated in our hearts. We may be in a state of mortal sin. In that case, we need to go to confession and then attempt reconciliation with that person. However, if our rupture with the other person is short-lived or due to impulse rather than deliberate and nursed by bitterness, then the "sign of peace" can act as a stimulus to reconcile at the earliest possible occasion.

How does the Eucharist help us here? We intend, with a firm resolution, to reconcile with that person with whom we are at odds. Then we receive Communion to strengthen us to love that person whom we find difficult, maybe impossible, to love. Jesus' loving presence makes our hearts able to love with a power beyond our normal ability. Strengthened by Christ's love in the sacrament, we then act upon our resolution by going to the person to ask for forgiveness or offer our forgiveness—or whatever else may be necessary and possible—to restore the relationship. We must remember that our actions cannot be conditioned on the other person's response. Even if that person does not respond favorably to our attempt at reconciliation, we should seek to make the attempt.

St. John Chrysostom offered this advice:

Does anyone have an enemy? Has he been wronged in a great way? Let him banish the enmity; let him keep in check his mind full of disorder that no one may be distracted or troubled. For you're about to receive the King under your roof in communion. As the King enters your soul, you should be in much tranquility, much silence, deep peace of thoughts. Have you been greatly wronged and cannot bear to let go of your anger? What greater, more severe wrong will you do yourself? Those things that your enemy has done, however great they be, are not so bad as you do to yourself if you are not reconciled to him but rather trample on the law of God.

Has he insulted you? So are you going to insult God? Tell me. Not being reconciled to the one who has caused you pain is not so much a matter of the one who defends himself as it is of the one who insults God who laid down these laws. So don't look at your fellow servant nor at the greatness of his offenses. Rather, as you put God and respect for him in your mind, examine this. The greater the act of violence you suffer in your soul in being reconciled to the one who has caused pain after being troubled by a thousand evils, that much more will you enjoy a greater honor from the God who commanded these things. And as you receive him here with much honor, so he will also receive you there with much glory, rewarding your obedience infinitely greater. May it be that we all attain to the grace of our Lord Jesus Christ and his love for humanity.[55]

John Chrysostom realized how painful our attempts at reconciliation can be. It takes enormous strength of character. But Holy Communion is an act of such great love that it is incompatible with deep hatred, because hatred of our fellow human beings kills the love of God within us. Such hatred can be overcome only by God's love dwelling within us. If we steadfastly refuse reconciliation with another person, it begins to eat away at our soul and destroys love in our hearts. ("What greater, more severe wrong will you do yourself?") We destroy ourselves even more by nurturing hate within us. But this Father of the Church also sympathizes with our struggle. He suggests that we look not at the greatness of the offense but at the greatness of God who wants us to reconcile. He even reminds us that the greater the transgression committed against us, the greater will be our victory over hate by seeking to forgive.

Reconciliation with our enemies and concern for the needs of our neighbor amounts to the same thing in Jesus' teaching when he calls us to emulate the perfect love of the heavenly Father:

> You have heard that it was said, "You shall love your neighbor and hate your enemy." But I say to you, love your enemies and pray for those who persecute you, so that you may be sons of your Father who is in heaven; for he makes his sun rise on the evil and on the good, and sends rain on the just and on the unjust. For if you love those who love you, what reward have you? Do not even the tax collectors do the same? And if you salute only your brethren, what more are you doing than others? Do not even the Gentiles do the same? You, therefore, must be perfect, as your heavenly Father is perfect. (Matt. 5:43–48)

Jesus' contemporaries had identified "neighbor" as their fellow Jews; that is why Jesus told the parable of the good Samaritan. Their "enemies" were the Romans, the Greeks, the Samaritans, and any others who were not them. The power of Jesus' teaching is that he called his contemporaries—as he calls us—back to the true meaning of the commandment by pointing back to the source of all love: the Father in heaven. His undiscriminating love for all is the model for our love. Receiving Jesus in the Eucharist calls us and empowers us to grow toward perfection by helping us focus on the one thing, the only thing, that really matters in the end: love.

Perhaps no one expressed this love better than a great Father of the Church, Augustine of Hippo. Speaking of those who are outside the Church and who oppose it, he pleads with his congregation to see that the eucharistic bread calls us to love beyond human power, to the kind of love that only Christ can instill within us:

And so, dear brothers, we entreat you on their behalf, in the name of the very source of our love, by whose milk we are nourished, and whose bread is our strength, in the name of Christ our Lord and his gentle love. For it is time now for us to show them great love and abundant compassion by praying to God for them. May he one day give them a clear mind to repent and to realize that they have nothing whatsoever to say against the truth; they have nothing now but sickness of their hatred, and the stronger they think they are, the weaker they become. We entreat you then to pray for them, for they are weak, given to the wisdom of the flesh, to fleshly and carnal things, but they are our brothers. . . . So pour out your hearts for them in prayer to God.[56]

AFTERWORD

The Divine Cycle of Love

Lovers of God. That is what we want to become. We should remember this tremendously comforting thought: the Father in heaven wants us to be his lovers even more than we want to be. This is why God established the divine cycle of love. Christ came from heaven to show the world the love of the Father. In the paschal mystery of his death and resurrection, he gives all we need to love God.

He gives himself to us in the Eucharist so that we may be able to show his love to the world. Those who accept Christ's love come to the Eucharist and ultimately return to the Father. From heaven to earth and back again. This is the divine cycle designed by God to lead human beings back to him, to bring us to our eternal home, because:

Love is our origin;
Love is our constant calling;
Love is our fulfillment in heaven.

GLOSSARY

Accidents: In medieval Thomistic philosophy, accidents are the observable characteristics of a thing. It contrasts with substances, which are unobservable. Thus, the accidents of bread and wine are color, texture, and taste. (See also *substance*.)

Adoration, Eucharistic: A practice of exposing the Blessed Sacrament in a monstrance, which allows the faithful to adore Christ in his sacramental species. The practice began sometime in the early Middle Ages of the Western Church. (See also *monstrance*.)

Anamnesis: The Greek word used by Paul (1 Cor. 11:25) and Luke (Luke 22:19) that is normally translated "remembrance" or "memory." But it means more than remembrance. It refers to a liturgical reenactment of the Last Supper, which Jesus commanded the apostles to perform.

Benediction: Originally the word simply meant blessing. In Catholic liturgy it refers to a short devotion, usually at the end of a period of adoration, when a priest leads the faithful in prayer and singing. The priest also blesses the people with the sacred host.

Body: In a eucharistic context, *body* refers to either Christ's humanity or the body of the Church, which is often called the mystical body.

Communion: In general, the word means sharing things in common. It came to be the main word describing the act of receiving

Christ in the Eucharist.

Concomitance: The dogma that is linked to transubstantiation that says that the *whole* Christ is present under both species of bread and wine as well as in every part. Christ's body is present in the wine and his blood is in the consecrated bread.

Consecration: The part of the Mass in which the priest becomes the voice of Jesus pronouncing "This is my body" and "This is my blood."

Contrition: Sorrow for sin. (See also *Perfect Contrition*.)

De fide: Literally "of the faith," it refers to the highest level of dogma in Catholic teaching. A *de fide* teaching must be believed.

Deification: The process of becoming more like God, called *theosis* in Greek. Deification happens when God communicates his divine nature to our human nature and elevates it beyond its human limitations. The Eucharist is the normal means to receive this divine life in Christ. Sometimes called divinization.

Didache: One of the earliest Christian documents outside the New Testament containing liturgical directives. It dates from the late first or early second century and testifies to the Church's faith in and practice of the Eucharist.

Disposition: A state of mind or heart on the part of the recipient of Holy Communion. The goal is always to have the proper dispositions of faith, hope, and love when receiving the Eucharist.

Divine Nature: The being of God, which is the source of all life and holiness. Since Jesus Christ is now inseparably and forever human and divine, he bestows his divine nature along with his human nature on those who receive him. Peter says those who belong to Christ are "partakers of the divine nature" (2 Pet. 1:4).

Domenicae Cenae: Pope John Paul II's 1980 apostolic letter on the Eucharist, which focused on the Last Supper. The English title is "On the Mystery and Worship of the Eucharist."

Ecclesia de Eucharistia: John Paul II's 2003 encyclical on the Eucharist in which he emphasizes the centrality of the Eucharist for the whole Church. The English title is "On the Eucharist in its Relationship to the Church."

Effect: The effect of the sacrament is the result it produces in the person receiving it. Thus, an increase in grace is a normal effect or result in the person who has received the Eucharist worthily.

Encyclical: A letter written and issued by the pope and usually addressed to the bishops of the world. In encyclicals, some aspect of Church teaching is presented.

Epiclesis: The invocation or calling down of the Holy Spirit in every Mass. The Spirit is the active agent who makes the bread and wine into the body and blood of Christ.

Eucharist: From the Greek meaning thanksgiving or gratitude, the term used since the very early Church to refer to the celebration of the sacrament.

Eucharistic Prayer: The part of the Mass, sometimes called the Canon of the Mass, that constitutes the main prayers offered to God the Father by the priest and the people.

Ex opere operato: Literally, "out of the work having been worked." The expression is used in Catholic teaching to describe how the Eucharist comes about from the words of Christ spoken by the priest. The words of Christ joined to the Holy Spirit's presence change the bread and wine into the substance of Christ's body and blood. This change does not depend on the worthiness or unworthiness of the priest. It objectively happens because of Christ's power to transform the elements.

Ex opere operantis: Literally, "out of the work of the one working." This phrase refers to the subjective dispositions of the priest and the people. The objective reality of Christ's bodily presence in the Eucharist does not depend on the priest or the people; however, the benefits both receive through Communion do depend on their subjective dispositions.

Florence, Council of: Ecumenical council of the 1430s and 1440s that reaffirmed the doctrine of transubstantiation. (See also *Lateran* and *Trent*.)

Grace: The unmerited favor of God by which he gives us a share in his very life. Since every member of the Trinity shares in this divine life, their presence in a human being conveys God's life to the human soul. Sharing in the divine life is both the goal and means by which we are saved.

Hoc est corpus meum: Latin words meaning "This is my body."

Host: From the Latin word meaning "offering," a host is the consecrated bread that has become the body of Christ.

Incarnation: The historically unique act of the second person of the Trinity becoming man. It is the foundational event of salvation history.

Incorporation: An effect of Christ's eucharistic presence by which he makes those who receive him more thoroughly the members of his body, the Church.

Justification: Being made just or righteous. An increase in righteousness comes from a faith-filled reception of the Eucharist as well as through other means of grace. (See *sanctification.*)

Koinonia: A Greek word meaning "communion," "fellowship," or "participation."

Lamb of God: An expression used for Jesus in John 1:29 that recalled the lamb of sacrifice used in the Passover. It is also used for Jesus in the book of Revelation.

Lateran Council, Fourth: The ecumenical council that took place in 1215 that determined that the dogma of transubstantiation should be held as definitive Catholic teaching.

Medicine of immortality: An expression first used by St. Ignatius of Antioch to mean that the Eucharist heals the body and soul to prepare them for eternal life.

Monstrance: A liturgical instrument used in exposition of the Blessed Sacrament. Monstrances are usually quite ornate with a small circular glass (lunette) in the middle where the consecrated host is placed for adoration by the faithful.

Mission: From the Latin for "sending." Christ, sent from the bosom of the Father, is the mission of God. Those who receive the Eucharist share in the mission of Christ.

Mortal sin: A sin that cuts off a person from active communion with God and the Church. For a sin to be mortal, it must entail grave matter, full knowledge by one who commits it that it is grave, and full consent of one's will.

Mystery: In a sacramental context, this term refers to an embodiment of God's presence and grace. The sacraments are mysteries because they continue the presence of Christ in the world and are beyond human capacity to understand. In the Eastern Catholic churches, the term *mystery* is used for the sacraments.

Participation: In a theological context, participation is sharing in the life of God. It means more than external reception of the Eucharist. It refers to the communication of God's life to the soul. Participation is one way to translate *koinonia*.

Paschal mystery: The passion, death, and resurrection of Christ. The faithful receive and share in the paschal mystery through the Eucharist.

Passover: The event in Israel's history in which God brought his people out of the slavery of Egypt. The people of Israel celebrated their redemption by having a sacred meal that foreshadowed the Last Supper, where Jesus instituted the Eucharist. It is sometimes referred to as *Pasch*.

Perfect contrition: A sorrow for sin solely because of the love of God rather than from fear of punishment by him.

Real Presence: A term of relatively recent origin to describe the Catholic belief that, in the Eucharist, the body, blood, soul, and divinity of Christ are truly present under the appearances of bread and wine.

Remedy: A solution to a problem. In a theological context, the Eucharist is a remedy against sin because it helps to overcome sin as medicine heals the body over time.

Sanctification: Being made holy. It normally occurs through prayer and the proper reception of the sacraments. The term is sometimes used as a synonym for justification and is sometimes distinguished from it. Like justification, sanctification can be both an event and a process.

Sacrament: An outward, physical sign instituted by Christ as a vessel of inward, spiritual grace. There are seven sacraments: baptism, reconciliation, Eucharist, confirmation, matrimony, holy orders, and anointing of the sick.

Sacrifice: A term applied to the Eucharist from the earliest times of the Church. The consecrated bread and wine are a sacrifice because Jesus and his death are fully present in them. The Eucharist is not an additional sacrifice to that of Calvary but the same sacrifice newly re-presented. The Eucharist both signifies and conveys what it signifies (that is, the body and blood of Christ).

Substance: In medieval Thomistic philosophy, a substance is that which makes something what it truly is. Substances are only known through accidents, which are the visible and tangible characteristics of a thing. Substances are unobservable. In the Eucharist, the substance of the bread and wine change into the substance of the body and blood of Christ. (See also *accidents*.)

Transubstantiation: The miraculous transformation of the *substances* of bread and wine into the substance of Christ's body and blood. This change takes place through the Holy Spirit joined to the words of consecration pronounced by the priest.

Trent, Council of: The ecumenical council of the sixteenth century that was called to respond the Protestant Reformation's claims and to reform the Church. With regard to the Eucharist, Trent reaffirmed and extended eucharistic dogma by emphasizing the Real Presence of Christ and the sacrificial nature of the Mass.

Viaticum: A Latin word meaning "food for the journey." Originally, it was applied to the Eucharist generally, but it later came to designate the last reception of the Eucharist before death.

Virtue: A Latin word originally meaning "power." Virtue is the moral power to do what is right. The three theological virtues are faith, hope, and charity (love). Ideally, growth in these virtues is a result or effect of Holy Communion.

Year of the Eucharist: John Paul II proclaimed October 2004 to October 2005 as an official year of the Eucharist for the whole Church.

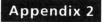

PRAYERS

ST. AMBROSE OF MILAN
Prayer before Communion

To the table of your delightful banquet, Lord Jesus Christ,
I a sinner come. I do not presume anything from my own merits,
But I trust your mercy and goodness.
I approach with fear and trembling,
For my heart and body are stained with many sins.
I do not guard my mind and tongue.

So, O loving God of majesty,
I, poor and distressed, quickly run to you
To be healed, to be under your protection.
I cannot sustain your judgment;
I long to have a Savior.

To you, Lord, I show my wounds
And uncover my shame.
I know my sins are many and great,
Which makes me afraid.
But I hope in your mercies,
Which are without number.

O look at me with your eyes of mercy,
Lord Jesus Christ, Eternal King, God and Man,
Crucified for man's sake.
Hear me who hopes in you.
Have mercy on me
Who is full of misery and sins.
You never cease to be the fount of mercy.

Hail, saving sacrifice,
Offered on the altar of the cross
For me and for all humanity.
Hail, noble and precious blood
Flowing from the side of the Crucified,
My Lord Jesus Christ,
Washing away the sins of the whole world.

Remember, Lord, your creature
Whom you have redeemed with your blood.
I repent of my sins and
Long to put right what I have done.

Take away from me, O loving Father,
All my iniquities and sins,
That with pure mind and body
I may be worthy to taste the holy of holies.

Grant that the holy offering
Of your body and blood that I intend to receive
May be the remission of my sins,
The perfect cleansing of my choices,
The banishing of my foul thoughts,
And the rebirth of good inclinations,
The saving efficacy of works pleasing to you,
The firmest possible defense against the attacks
Of my enemies of soul and body.
Amen.

ST. THOMAS AQUINAS

Prayer before Communion

Eternal, Almighty God,
I come to the sacrament of your only begotten Son,
Our Lord Jesus Christ.
I come like the sick to the physician of life,
Unclean to the fount of mercy,
Blind to the light of eternal brilliance,
Poor and needy to the Master of heaven and earth.

I ask from the abundance of your immense wealth
To kindly cure my sickness,
Wash my filth, illumine my blindness,
Enrich my poverty, clothe my nakedness
That I may receive the bread of angels,
The king of kings and lord of lords
With such reverence and humility,
With such contrition and devotion,
With such purity and faith,
With such purpose and resolution
As is good for saving my soul.

Grant to me to receive not only the sign
Of the Lord's body and blood
But also its reality and power.

O God, kindest of all,
Give me the body of your only begotten Son,
Our Lord Jesus Christ,
That was drawn from the Virgin Mary's womb,
To receive it so I may be embodied in his mystical body
And counted among his members.

O most loving Father,
Convey to me your beloved Son whom I
Now intend to receive in this life
That, standing face to face,
I may forever contemplate him
Who lives and reigns for ever and ever.
Amen.

St. Thomas Aquinas

Prayer after Communion

Lord, Holy Father, all-powerful and eternal God,
I, who am a sinner, your unworthy servant, thank you
That you have kindly satisfied me
With the precious body and blood of your Son,
Our Lord Jesus Christ.
This was not because of any merits of my own.
It flowed solely from your mercy.
I beg that this Holy Communion will not be for me
An accusation leading to punishment
But a saving plea for forgiveness.

May it be for me the armor of faith
And the shield of good will.
May it be for me
An emptying of my faults;
An extermination of evil desire and lust;
A growth of all virtues:
Love and patience,
Humility and obedience;
A firm defense against attacks of all enemies,
Both visible and invisible;
A perfect quieting of my disturbances,
Both fleshly and spiritual;
A firm adherence to you,

The one and true God;
And a happy consummation of my goal.
I beg you that you would be pleased to lead me,
A sinner, to that ineffable banquet
Where you, with your Son and the Holy Spirit,
Are for all your saints
True light,
Complete satisfaction,
Perpetual joy,
Consummate beauty,
And perfect happiness.
Through Christ our Lord.
Amen.

ST. THOMAS AQUINAS

Adoro Te Devote

Hidden God, devoutly I adore you
Who lies under these forms truly.
My heart submits to you,
For it melts on seeing you surely.

Sight, touch, taste fall short in you.
Only hearing believes completely.
I believe what the Son of God says,
Nothing than from the Word of truth more truly.

Only deity was hidden on the cross;
Here humanity hides with no loss.
Believing both with mouth professing,
I ask only with the thief confessing.
Amen.

St. Bonaventure

Prayer before or after Communion

O sweetest Jesus,
Pierce the sinews and crevices of my soul
With the kindest, saving wound of your love,
With a truly calm, holy, and apostolic charity,
That my soul may languish and melt.
From its constant untarnished love and desire for you,
May my soul long and even faint in your courts;
May it seek to be as nothing with you.

Grant my soul to hunger for you, the bread of angels,
The refreshment of holy souls, our daily, supersubstantial bread,
That has all sweetness, taste, and every sweet delicacy.
May my heart always hunger for and feed on you, whom angels
desire to see.
May it be filled with the sweetness of tasting you.
May the very depths of my soul always thirst for you,
The fount of life,
The fount of wisdom and knowledge,
The fount of eternal light
That burns with pleasure
And is the wealth of God's house.

May my soul always encompass you, seek you, find you,
Stretch itself out for you, arrive at you.
May my soul meditate on you, speak of you.
May it do everything for the praise and glory of your name,
With humility and discretion,
With love and delight,
With ease and affection,
With perseverance to the end.

All this, that you alone may always be my hope,
My complete trust, my wealth, my delight, my beauty,
My joy, my rest and tranquility, my peace, my sweetness,
My fragrance, my food, my refreshment,
My help, my wisdom, my portion, my possession, my treasure
house
In whom my mind and heart are fixed, firm and unshakably
rooted.
Amen.

Appendix 3

WHERE TO LEARN MORE: RECOMMENDED READING

Bouyer, Louis. *The Eucharist.* Notre Dame, Ind.: University of Notre Dame Press, 1968.

> An in-depth look at liturgies in the history of the Church. It shows both the diversity among liturgies and the continuity through the centuries.

Eymard, St. Peter Julian. *How to Get More out of Holy Communion.* Manchester, N.H.: Sophia Institute Press, 2000.

> Selections from one of the greatest eucharistic saints, and the founder of the Congregation of the Blessed Sacrament.

Gaudoin-Parker, Michael L. *The Real Presence through the Ages.* New York: Alba House, 1993.

> A collection of original sources of great saints and theologians on the Eucharist from St. Ignatius of Antioch to Blessed Teresa of Calcutta.

Groeschel, Benedict J. and James Monti. *In the Presence of Our Lord: The History, Theology and Psychology of Eucharistic Devotion.* Huntington, Ind.: Our Sunday Visitor, 1997.

> An informative, enlightening survey of eucharistic devotion.

O'Connor, James. *The Hidden Manna.* San Francisco: Ignatius Press, 1988.

A survey of the Church's teaching on the Eucharist from the beginning to the present.

STUDY QUESTIONS

Answers are at the end of the questions.

1. What is the original meaning of the word *Eucharist* (*eucharistia* in Greek)?

2. What reasons can you give for why Jesus wanted to eat the Passover meal with his disciples?

3. List the three themes of the Passover that can be gleaned from Exodus chapter twelve?
   A. _____
   B. _____
   C. _____

4. What in Jesus' words and actions at the Last Supper indicate that he was establishing the New Covenant with the people of God?

5. The question from St. Thomas Aquinas on page XX of *The Eucharist for Beginners: Sacrament, Sacrifice, and Communion* says that Christ revealed his love in his Passion (that is, in suffering and death). What connection do you see between the Passion of Christ and the Eucharist?

6. Explain how the Eucharist is "the source and summit" of the Christian life?

7. In what ways does the Eucharist demonstrate Jesus' love for us?

8. How is the phrase "Do this in memory of me" often misunderstood by Christians?

9. Explain the Greek and Hebrew backgrounds for the meaning of *anamnesis*. How is *anamnesis* more than "remembering"?

10. How does 1 Corinthians 10:16–17 imply the Real Presence of Christ in the Eucharist? What relationship between the Eucharist and the Church is expressed in these verses?

11. Why did Jesus perform the miracle of the feeding of the five thousand?

12. What Greek verb in John 6:23 indicates that John wanted us to see a connection between the feeding of the five thousand and the Eucharist?

13. What does Jesus mean by "the bread from heaven" in John 6?

14. What statement does St. Ignatius of Antioch make that shows that he believed in the Real Presence of Jesus Christ in the Eucharist?

15. According to St. Ignatius, what makes for a valid Eucharist?

16. What did St. Justin Martyr say were the conditions for receiving the Eucharist?

17. How did St. Justin express the relationship between the Incarnation (the Word becoming flesh) and the Eucharist?

18. On what authority did St. Cyril of Jerusalem base his distinction between the appearances of bread and wine and the reality of Christ's body and blood?

19. What does the dogma of transubstantiation mean?

20. How is transubstantiation the opposite of what normally happens in nature?

21. Once transubstantiation takes place, what parts of Christ are present under the appearances of bread and wine?

22. When was the dogma of transubstantiation first officially proclaimed?

23. How did St. Ambrose, in the fourth century, express the essence of transubstantiation even though he does not use that word? To what does Ambrose compare the transformation that takes place in the Eucharist?

24. What is the ultimate reason for believing in transubstantiation?

25. How and why is Jesus' use of words different from an ordinary human being's use of words?

26. Name three documents from early Christianity that show that the Church has always believed in the Eucharist as a sacrifice.

27. In Malachi 1:11, how does the phrase "from the rising of the sun to its setting" indicate the universality of the sacrifice of the Eucharist?

28. Why is it important to emphasize the sacrificial nature of the Eucharist, and what is left out if we fail to stress this?

29. In what way does Jesus act as both priest and victim in the Mass?

30. What does Hebrews 10:10 teach about the connection between the body of Jesus and our growth in holiness (that is, sanctification)?

31. If Jesus offered his life as a sacrifice on the cross once and for all, why do we still need to offer the Eucharist as a sacrifice?

32. How does Eucharist not take away from Jesus' sacrifice on the cross? How is it the same sacrifice as on Calvary?

33. What is meant by saying that the sacrifice of every Mass is really the same sacrifice?

34. How does the sacrifice of the Eucharist show the depths of Jesus' love?

35. Why is asking God for mercy appropriate at Communion time? How is God's mercy related to contrition, or sorrow for sin?

36. What does receiving the Eucharist imply about one's attitude toward fellow believers?

37. What are some ways a person might "partake unworthily" of the body and blood of the Lord?

38. What is a mortal sin, and how does a person know when he has committed one?

39. A person who has committed a mortal sin should do what?

40. What are some reasons for the fast before Communion?

41. Why should the time after receiving Holy Communion be spent in recollected silence and meditation?

42. What is the meaning of sanctification and of justification? How are the two related?

43. What is the relationship between baptism and the Eucharist as far as the Christian life is concerned?

44. According to the Council of Florence, what are some of the effects of Communion?

45. How necessary is the Eucharist to our growth in holiness? How would you explain the holiness of Christians who never receive the true body and blood of Christ?

46. What does *theosis* mean?

47. What is the essence of holiness? Normally, how long does it take to achieve holiness?

48. What is the meaning of the Mass in terms of this statement: We bring God gifts, and he gives us gifts, which are then given back to him?

49. What is the greatest gift we can give to God?

50. According to St. Thomas Aquinas, what power does the Eucharist have?

51. How can the Eucharist help a person overcome evil?

52. What do the verses from John's Gospel on page XX of *The Eucharist for Beginners: Sacrament, Sacrifice, and Communion* teach about the reasons the Son of God came into the world?

53. In what way is the scriptural phrase "body of Christ" used to describe the Church more than a simple analogy?

54. What does it mean that you are what you receive in the Eucharist and you become more so by receiving it?

55. If, by receiving the Eucharist faithfully, we can grow more in love with Jesus, how can that love show itself in our mission? What kind of heart should a Catholic seek to develop?

56. How does our suffering help fulfill Christ's mission in the world?

57. Why is eucharistic adoration important?

58. What is the ultimate source of grace in the Catholic life?

59. Why is the Eucharist called "the sacrament of unity"?

60. What do the eucharistic prayers of the Mass suggest about the importance of unity in a Catholic view of the Church?

61. What do the verses in 1 Corinthians 10:14–17 teach about the relationship between partaking of the Eucharist and the growth of the Church?

62. How do bread and wine reflect both the diversity and unity of the Church?

63. Explain what it means to say that the Eucharist is the connection between the paschal mystery and the Church?

64. How important is unity with the ordained pastors of the Church? What historical evidence shows that disunity with the Church's leaders has always been a problem?

65. What is wrong with the idea that the Church is only a loose body of Christian believers, and that it need not have a common governmental structure?

66. If the Church had no visible head representing Christ, what would that imply about Jesus?

67. Why is it a contradiction to pray for the pope and our bishops in every Mass but then disobey them?

68. What does receiving the Eucharist say about our faith?

69. How does properly receiving the Eucharist show our love of God?

70. How does loving one's neighbor relate to the Eucharist?

71. How can our daily lives become more and more eucharistic?

72. How we can "see" Jesus in the Eucharist and in the poor?

73. Who are the poor in your community, and how can you serve them in ways that bring them to the Eucharist?

74. Why is receiving the Eucharist incompatible with an unwillingness to forgive?

75. What is the Sign of Peace during Mass supposed to remind us of, and to what moral obligation does it call us?

76. According to St. John Chrysostom's sixth homily, how is a lack of forgiveness a worse wound than that which you have already received?

77. How should receiving the Eucharist affect how we think and feel about those who are not members of the Church?

STUDY ANSWERS

1. Thanksgiving or gratitude.

2. In his sorrow, Jesus knew he would not be with his disciples much longer. Jesus also loved them so much that he wanted to establish the Eucharist as a gift as he was about to depart his earthly life.

3. A. Annual celebration
   B. Sacrifice
   C. Purity

4. The phrase "This is the cup of my blood," which alluded to the blood of the covenant mentioned in the Old Testament. Jesus also established the people of the New Covenant at the Passover meal, which showed his linking the Church to ancient Israel.

5. All sacraments embody the Passion of Christ but especially the Eucharist, since it is Jesus in his fullest form in this world.

6. Since the Eucharist is Jesus Christ, it takes us back to Christ as the source of graces and points us to him as the goal of our life.

7. The Eucharist is the gift of Jesus' own life given to and for us.

8. Many mistakenly think Jesus was just telling us to remember him in an act of mental recollection. This is not the case; he is asking—and giving us—much more.

9. The Hebrew and Greek backgrounds of *anamnesis* suggest that he was directing his apostles to reenact the Last Supper to bring his presence into the world. *Anamanesis* is primarily a liturgical act.

10. We can have communion (*koinonia*) with the body and blood of Christ only if he is really present in the Eucharist. The Eucharist feeds the Church body with the sacramental body of Christ and thereby makes it more unified.

11. The act demonstrated Jesus' sensitivity to people's needs while at the same time teaching his disciples to trust in him whenever they are in tough circumstances in the future, even when their resources are obviously inadequate. Foremost, as the *Catechism of the Catholic Church* says, "When the Lord says the blessing, breaks and distributes the loaves through his disciples to the multitude, [this] prefigure[s] the superabundance of this unique bread of his Eucharist."[57]

12. *Eucharisteo.*

13. Jesus contrasts the manna of the Old Testament with himself as the true "bread from heaven."

14. "Be diligent to employ only one Eucharist. For there is only one flesh of our Lord Jesus Christ and there is only one cup for unity in his blood."

15. A eucharistic celebration that is performed or authorized by the bishop.

16. A person must be baptized and believe what the Church teaches.

17. The Eucharist is like another Incarnation or, seen in its fullness, a continuation of the original Incarnation.

18. "On the Lord's own declaration."

19. Transubstantiation means that the substance of the bread and wine becomes the substance of the body and blood of Christ.

20. In nature, accidents typically change while the substance remains. In transubstantiation, the opposite occurs. The substance changes while the accidents of the bread and wine remain.

21. Every part of the whole Christ (body, blood, soul, and divinity) is present in every part of the bread and wine.

22. In 1215 at the Fourth Lateran Council.

23. St. Ambrose taught that the transformation of the bread and wine into Christ's body and blood was a miraculous change effected by the Savior's words. He compares it to Elijah's words that bring down fire from heaven.

24. There are many reasons including scriptural teaching and authority of the Church, but ultimately it is because Jesus said it. "This is my body."

25. Being God, Jesus can use words performatively—that is, he can make them do what they signify.

26. *The Didache*, St. Justin Martyr's *Dialogue with Trypho the Jew*, and St. Irenaeus's *Against Heresies*.

27. The expression "from the rising to the setting of the sun" refers to both geographical and temporal universality (everywhere and always).

28. A perfect sacrifice is necessary for us to be acceptable to God. If we fail to emphasize the Mass as the sacrifice of Jesus, we ultimately downplay the saving death of Jesus.

29. Jesus uses the mouth of an ordained priest to speak his own words, "This is my body." Since Christ is fully present under the appearances of bread and wine, his saving death is also present in which he offers himself again to the Father as victim for our sins.

30. That our holiness is found in the body of Jesus.

31. The Eucharist applies the death of Jesus that was accomplished once to his people in the Mass. We need ongoing applications of his death for us to forgive our sins and to liberate us from sin.

32. Jesus is not "re-sacrificed." His original sacrifice is applied to the Church by being brought down from heaven again.

33. Every Mass consecrates the bread and wine and transforms them into Christ's body and blood. But this is the same body and blood of Jesus that are in heaven. All Masses on earth are embodiments of the one heavenly Mass.

34. It reminds us of Christ's great gift of self.

35. Because we are in need of God's mercy to receive Christ properly in Communion. God always hears a contrite heart crying out to him. We should be like the good thief who asked Jesus, "Remember me when you come into your kingdom" (Luke 23:42).

36. It implies that we are at one with fellow Christians and that there are no obstacles to loving them in our hearts.

37. Unworthy partaking arises from being in a state of mortal sin in which we have severed ourselves from the love of God.

38. A mortal sin is a sin that cuts us off from active communion with God and from the Church. The guilt can be removed only by the sacrament of reconciliation (going to confession). A person has committed a mortal sin if three conditions are met: the person knows the sin was a grave matter; the person knew it was wrong; and the person commits the sin with the deliberate consent of his will.

39. He should go to confession to be reconciled to God and to the Church through the merciful ministry of the priest. No one should receive Communion in a state of mortal sin.

40. The fast is to prepare us to receive Christ in the Eucharist worthily. Refraining from food and drink forces us to think consciously of the importance of the communion into which we are about to enter.

41. To allow the presence of Christ to sink deeply into our consciousness.

42. Sanctification is growth in holiness. Justification is being right with God. They are two terms describing the same process of growth in grace. As we come to have God's presence more in our lives, we are enabled to grow in righteousness and thereby become more justified.

43. Baptism begins our Christian life by cleansing us from the guilt of original sin and actual sins we have committed up to that point. In baptism we receive the Holy Spirit and become members of the Church. The Eucharist is the ongoing nourishment of our Christian life.

44. Communion feeds us spiritually just as natural food feeds our bodies.

45. Since the Eucharist feeds us with Christ himself, it is necessary to receive it. Jesus himself said that he is "the way, and the truth, and the life" (John 14:6). Without him we cannot be saved. Even though the Eucharist is Jesus' normal chosen way to communicate his life to us, he can and does give of himself to people who have never had the opportunity to receive the Eucharist.

46. Divinization, or becoming more godlike.

47. Holiness consists mainly in loving God as he first loved us. Normally it takes a lifetime.

48. The Mass is a circle of love from God to man and back to God.

49. Our love.

50. To give growth in virtue and the power to avoid sin.

51. Because Christ through the Eucharist is fully present in the person who properly receives him, he gives that person the desire to avoid sin and to do good.

52. To rescue us from eternal damnation and to grant us eternal life. All this flowed from God's love.

53. The Church is Christ's body because Christ mystically communicates his divinity and humanity to the members of the Church.

54. The recipient of the Eucharist receives the body of Christ and becomes more deeply a part of the mystical body of Christ, the Church.

55. A heart of sharing the riches of Christ with the world.

56. By suffering of various kinds, we share in the Passion of Christ and bring others to Jesus' cross as we lift them to him.

57. It allows the sacramental presence of Christ to penetrate profoundly into our consciousness and so transform us.

58. Christ himself.

59. The Eucharist signifies the unity of the Church and engenders our unity with the Church when we receive it.

60. Unity is one of the four essential marks of the Church and is therefore of the highest importance (the other marks being that the Church is holy, catholic, and apostolic).

61. The unity of the Church can grow stronger through Holy Communion.

62. Bread is made of many grains and wine is produced from many grapes. Yet, once made, bread and wine are whole units. The Church, too, is made up of many elements brought together into one.

63. The Church and its members can be saved only through sharing in Christ's paschal mystery. Since the Eucharist embodies the paschal mystery, it communicates the benefits of Christ's Passion to the Church.

64. It is absolutely important. Historical evidence includes the writings of Paul, St. Ignatius of Antioch, and St. John Chrysostom as well as the rupture caused by the Protestant Reformation.

65. Such a conception in effect denies the structure of the Church taught in the New Testament.

66. That he did not provide an instrument for Christian unity.

67. To pray for unity with the pope and our bishops implies a willingness to obey their legitimate leadership.

68. It says that we desire to be in union with the whole Church under the guidance of the magisterium.

69. It shows our desire to love God as he has loved us and that we want to be united with God on his terms. He is God and we are his creatures.

70. One cannot truly love God unless he loves his neighbor (1 John 4:11, 20).

71. By living consciously in the presence of Christ, whom we receive in the Eucharist.

72. By faith we see more than meets the eye.

73. Reader's answer.

74. The Eucharist implies receiving the forgiveness of Christ and a willingness to pursue reconciliation with our fellow human beings.

75. Of our need to be at peace with all others (Rom. 12:18).

76. Unwillingness to forgive estranges us from the love of God and hardens our hearts.

77. It should engender compassion within us and motivate us to work for the salvation of others.

ENDNOTES

MAIN TEXT

[1] St. Thomas Aquinas, *On the Feast of the Body of Christ.*

[2] Eucharistic Prayer II.

[3] Eucharistic Prayer III.

[4] St. Ignatius of Antioch, *Letter to the Philadelphians* 4:1.

[5] *Catechism of the Catholic Church* 1345.

[6] St. Justin Martyr, *First Apology* 66.

[7] St. Cyril of Jerusalem, *Catechetical Lectures* 6.

[8] Eucharistic Prayer II.

[9] Eucharistic Prayer III.

[10] St. Ambrose of Milan, *On the Mysteries* 52.

[11] Council of Trent, session 13, ch. 4, 1551.

[12] *Didache* 14.

[13] St. Justin Martyr, *Dialogue with Trypho the Jew* 41, 1–3.

[14] St. Irenaeus of Lyons, *Against Heresies* 4, 17, 5.

[15] St. Cyprian of Carthage, *Epistle 63.*

[16] Council of Trent, *Decree on the Sacrifice of the Mass.*

[17] Second Vatican Council, *Lumen Gentium* 11.

[18] John Paul II, *Ecclesia de Euchaistia* 11, 12; cf. CCC 1382.

[19] Eucharistic Prayer III.

[20] CCC 1388.
[21] Ibid., 1385.
[22] *Code of Canon Law* 916.
[23] CCC 1855.
[24] John Paul II, *Reconciliatio et Paenitentia* 17, 2.
[25] CCC 2066, 2067.
[26] St. Cyril of Jerusalem, *Mystagogy* 5:22.
[27] St. John Chrysostom, *Homily 6*.
[28] St. Thomas Aquinas, *Summa Theologiae* III.79.1.
[29] St. Ambrose of Milan, *On the Sacraments* 5.
[30] Prayer over the Gifts.
[31] Eucharistic Prayer III.
[32] CCC 1030–1032.
[33] St. John Chrysostom, *Catechesis* 3, 13.
[34] St. Bonaventure, *Breviloquim* 6, 9, 3.
[35] St. Augustine, *Epistle* 12.
[36] Pius XII, *Mystici Corporis Christi* 12.
[37] Paul VI, *Mysterium Fidei* 67.
[38] Eucharistic Prayer I.
[39] Eucharistic Prayer II.
[40] Eucharistic Prayer III.
[41] Eucharistic Prayer III.
[42] *Didache* 9.
[43] *Didache* 10.
[44] St. Cyprian of Carthage, *Epistle* 69, 4.
[45] St. Fulgentius, *Epistle* 12.
[46] John Paul II, *Ecclesia de Eucharistia* 23.
[47] LG 1.
[48] Second Vatican Council, *Unitatis Redintegratio* 5.
[49] See also John Paul II's encyclical letter *Ut Unum Sint* 6.
[50] Eucharistic Prayer II.
[51] Leo XIII, *Satis Cognitum* 3.
[52] LG 11.
[53] St. John Chrysostom, *Homily 50*.
[54] St. Justin Martyr, *First Apology* 65–67.
[55] St. John Chrysostom, *Homily 6*.

[56] St. Augustine, *A Discourse on the Psalms.*
[57] *Catechism of the Catholic Church* 1335.

SIDEBAR TEXT

[1] John Paul II, Ecclesia de Eucharistia 61.
[2] John Paul II, Ecclesia de Eucharistia 15.
[3] Catechism of the Catholic Church 1131.
[4] St. Gregory the Great, Homily on the Gospels 14.
[5] St. Ignatius of Antioch, Letter to the Smyrnaeans 8:1–2.
[6] St. Cyril of Jerusalem, Catechetical Lectures 9.
[7] Council of Florence, Decree for the Armenians.
[8] St. Ambrose of Milan, On the Priesthood 4, 3.
[9] John Paul II, Ecclesia de Eucharistia 13; cf. Second Vatican Council, Lumen Gentium 11.
[10] John Paul II, Dominicae Cenae 7.
[11] St. Gregory the Great, Moralia on Job 13, 21–23.
[12] St. Ignatius of Antioch, Letter to the Ephesians 4.
[13] St. Ignatius of Antioch, Letter to the Philadelphians 4:1.
[14] Pius XII, Mystici Corporis Christi 40, 41.
[15] John Paul II, Dominicae Cenae 6.
[16] Leo the Great, Sermon 10.